The Subtle Side of Teaching

The Subtle Side of Teaching

Small Things That Make a Big Difference in Your Classroom

Nathan O. Buonviri

ROWMAN & LITTLEFIELD
Lanham • Boulder • New York • London

Published by Rowman & Littlefield
An imprint of The Rowman & Littlefield Publishing Group, Inc.
4501 Forbes Boulevard, Suite 200, Lanham, Maryland 20706
www.rowman.com

6 Tinworth Street, London SE11 5AL, United Kingdom

British Library Cataloguing in Publication Information Available

Library of Congress Cataloging-in-Publication Data

ISBN 9781475854305 (cloth : alk. paper)
ISBN 9781475854312 (pbk. : alk. paper)
ISBN 9781475854329 (electronic)

∞™ The paper used in this publication meets the minimum requirements of American National Standard for Information Sciences—Permanence of Paper for Printed Library Materials, ANSI/NISO Z39.48-1992.

For Maria, Carlo, Paolo, and Matteo

Contents

Contents

Foreword

It's axiomatic that one must be a student as long as one lives. Living requires learning—conscious and deliberate as well as unconscious and by unintended consequences.

It's likewise axiomatic that one is a teacher as long as one lives. That is to say that others inspire, inform, and mentor us well beyond the years of formal schooling—both by setting a good or a bad example—on a daily basis. We relentlessly watch each other—learning and teaching.

It's also axiomatic that nobody learns more than a teacher. What the best teachers have to teach is a passion for learning, as is the case for the author of this book, Nathan Buonviri. It is said that the mediocre teacher tells; the good teacher explains; the superior teacher demonstrates; and the great teacher inspires. And I was inspired by Antoine de Saint-Exupéry, who wrote, *"If you want to build a ship, don't drum up people together to collect wood and don't assign them tasks and work, but rather teach them to long for the endless immensity of the sea."*

This book and its author embrace these ideas and values.

With very little adaptation, this book could be an inspirational manual for a flourishing life—for all those who understand that they are both students and teachers as long as they live—in the classroom of the world.

Robert Fulghum
Author of
All I Really Need to Know I Learned in Kindergarten

Preface

Some time ago, I was born into the home of two teachers. Dad enjoyed a career in high school math and Mom taught quite the variety, including Earth Science, Home Economics, British Literature, and her own preschool, to name a few. I distinctly remember, from my very early years, that conversations at the dinner table focused on decisions at faculty meetings, humorous student quotes, personal reflections on teaching time and energy, and spontaneous reflections on what made it all somehow work day after day.

I was vaguely interested in those conversations at the time, as engaged as any average kid might be in his parents' work lives, maybe less so. What I remember clearly, though, is that it all just seemed to make sense. Their accounts of school circumstances, interactions with students, colleagues, and administrators, and personal development as teachers resonated with me in a tangible way, especially as I embarked on formal schooling myself as a kindergartener. As my own high school graduation, college education, professional teaching, and graduate studies came and went, I grew in the official knowledge and skills of proper classroom pedagogy, eventually yielding the teacher training that I now offer to university students. All the while, though, I also recognized simple seeds that were planted those many years ago, small but profound ways of looking a little deeper at life as a teacher.

Throughout my professional work in education, I have continued to notice relatively subtle things that can make all the difference in a teacher's day. I fully recognize and affirm how important the explicit, observable training we offer our educators in pre-service and in-service training is, but I also acknowledge those sneaky little momentary flashes of insight that fly under the radar all the time—those unspoken choices we make, unnoticed assumptions we carry, inner battles we fight, and personal perspectives we embrace

or discard, all of which may be completely invisible to others and, unfortunately, sometimes even to ourselves.

This book is about us, about each of us teachers taking a deeper look, as
clearly and frequently as possible, into our life's work. The essays that follow
derive from decades of learning, teaching, researching, coaching others, and
learning some more. Each chapter is an attempt to trigger something in you
that perhaps you have not had the opportunity or the time to explore. Each
depends on your unique background, interest level, focus of attention, and
motivation. Each targets something specific that has arisen enough times, in
enough situations, to beg a closer look.

Perhaps a few timeless classroom instructions will set us off on the right
foot as we begin:

Please put your pencils down.
Clear off your desk. And your mind.
Listen carefully to each of the prompts that follows.
Think clearly and thoroughly as you formulate your response to each.
Good luck. We're so proud of you.

Acknowledgments

I hereby acknowledge *all* of my teachers over the past many years, for their profound influence on me as a person, student, teacher, and author of this book:

parents
siblings
extended family
school teachers
librarians
coaches
pack leaders
security guards
cafeteria staff
maintenance personnel
restaurant supervisors
music directors
authors
conference speakers
landlords
colleagues
principals
deans
personal mentors

A detailed list of names and explanations for this gesture of gratitude would be completely overwhelming. Instead, I send all of you a silent word of thanks for your willingness to show others the way.

Chapter 1

Your Environment

PURPOSE, NOT YOU, SHOULD RUN YOUR CLASSROOM

It's tough to be in charge all the time, calling the shots, handling the challenges, and leading the way. Many days, teachers feel we are giving all we have and still sprinting to keep up. Our ability to consistently run our classrooms well depends on a number of factors, including organization skills, personal health, attitude, quick thinking, and general job satisfaction. Often overlooked, however, is what is behind all of that: Who, exactly, is running this classroom? Is it really possible for you to be everywhere at once, supervising every student move and controlling all environmental factors? Of course not. All teachers must come to terms with the fact that our classrooms are not fully "ours." We take responsibility for the overall direction of the course, preparing the way and helping students through it, but instead of envisioning ourselves "running" every detail of student learning we could hand the reins over to a powerful partner—purpose.

"Third party" is a fascinating term used frequently in manufacturing, business, and even education to refer to a separate entity that contributes to an interaction between two original parties. Third-party affiliates can cause problems, of course, but mostly they contribute valuable assets to a relationship that the original entities could not muster themselves. They may provide objectivity because of their relatively low level of interest in the relationship itself. They may provide a fresh perspective due to their lack of history with the original partners. They may serve in a supervisory or assessment role, providing a thorough investigation of an institution or event, or producing a certification required by policy or law.

A great example of a third party at work in education is the standardized exam. For instance, national Advanced Placement course exams introduce a third-party quality control on instruction and learning in courses across school districts and states. Teachers and students can access valuable resources to guide their progress through the course, checking regularly whether they are on track to be fully prepared for the exam by the end. If not monitored closely, this approach could simply become "teaching to the test," but if handled wisely, it serves to motivate both teacher and students to put forth their best work at a challenging pace. In fact, this third party can be the impetus for teacher and students to unite, focusing together on a common goal and using it to coordinate their efforts.

Just think of it: a slight mental shift from teacher and students operating from two separate camps to teacher and students truly teaming up toward a clear purpose. At the moment, what would you state as the central purpose of each of your classes? Do students know it? *Really* know it? Are they on board? Do you see yourself and them on the same team? Do they? Have you ever discussed the purpose that guides your classroom as a clear and tangible third party, something that all of you can get behind together?

A nation's constitution can serve a wonderful third-party role, providing structure and space for government leaders, justices, lawyers, and public servants to do their work fully supported on behalf of informed citizens. Have you established some sense of constitution for your classroom—something that both you and students can appeal to when tricky situations arise? Have you clarified the priorities in your room such that most daily details are solved quickly and easily in the shadow of the bigger picture? Letting purpose run your classroom may feel like abdication at first, but it can reduce an enormous amount of unnecessary weight from the shoulders of the one trying to run the whole show. An extra step toward clarity of purpose right now can have large and lasting effects in the future.

KEY IDEAS:

- Let purpose be your partner.
- Find "third-party" factors that can help unify the efforts in your classroom.

IN QUALITY CLASSROOMS, STUDENTS ARE USUALLY DOING MUCH MORE THAN TEACHERS

School is for students, not for teachers. If we are truly committed to this "serving" profession, we must realize this early on and remind ourselves of it constantly. The priority placed on students in your room is evidenced by the age-old truth that actions speak louder than words—louder than words like "student-centered learning."

Hopefully, this educational cliché sounds slightly ridiculous as you read it. *Of course* learning must be student-centered; how could it be anything else?! Well, the phrase came about precisely because there is a possibility that "learning" could be construed otherwise, namely as something that the teacher somehow imparts. We teachers take our work quite seriously, but we cannot call it teaching if there was no learning, and students have to actually *do* the learning. How do we gauge the relative priority placed on students and teacher in a classroom? By the number and quality of actions each produces.

Teachers may agree conceptually that students' overt actions and real experiences are what produce the most effective and lasting learning, but we sometimes forget it in the heat of the moment. We may become momentarily enamored with the sound of our own voice or convinced that our example is just too perfect to pass up. We may wish to maintain the entire class's focus or perhaps we are slightly afraid of classroom management issues. We might feel irresponsible or lazy if we trim back our activity and let students find their own way on a given task. All of these may be appropriate and helpful perspectives once in a while, but when allowed to fester frequently they can tip the teacher-student balance dramatically and undesirably. Tracking the observable actions of teachers and the observable actions of students can help us keep ourselves balanced, or better yet, unbalanced in the students' favor.

Have you ever heard an educational conference speaker express a similar sentiment only to follow with something like "Of course, I'm not doing a very good job of teaching right now with my PowerPoint lecture [laughter]"? Why not go ahead and change that? In each of our own learning environments, are there ways we can prompt more frequent and sustained student action? All too often, an "active" learning environment is interpreted as a situation in which students are highly attentive—"actively listening" or "actively taking notes." The real action, engaging, colorful, and interesting as it may be, is still mostly assumed by the teacher or some other source. This classroom dynamic might not be a frequent problem for you, but does it ever happen in your room? Could the balance be improved even more?

Enough lecture for now. In the spirit of this essay, it's your turn. Take a few moments to list feasible, responsible, and defensible ways that you could reduce the actions you supply and increase the actions students take in your room. Discover how you might actually *do* less so that they can *do* more, all day every day. You'll be glad you did!

KEY IDEAS:

- Monitor the balance between your actions and students' actions.
- Consider giving up some of your favorite moves to make room for student contributions.

A CLASS OF STUDENTS SHOULD BE MUCH GREATER THAN THE SUM OF ITS PARTS

While on my daily walk yesterday, I had the opportunity to watch a roofing crew do their thing on a neighbor's house. During the few minutes I observed, one person was nailing new shingles quickly and cleanly in an orderly pattern. Another was cutting and installing all of the flashing. A third was finishing up the removal of previous material from the structure, and the fourth was disposing of debris into the dumpster and providing tools and materials right on time for the first three.

As the four of them worked together, I realized right away that their approach was producing faster and better results than would have occurred if all of them did exactly the same job, tackling a little bit of each part of the work. Imagine the nailer putting everything down to go get a new pack of shingles every five minutes, or the flashing guy making a run to the dumpster every time he cut off a piece of discard metal. They each played their respective roles in a focused way producing a fine roof as efficiently as possible. The whole of the crew was much greater than the sum of its four parts.

Each of those four jobs could get highly tedious so perhaps they rotate tasks from roof to roof. Doing so would keep their work fresh and interesting, and also help all of them maintain a clear and helpful sense of the scope of the whole operation. Rotating tasks can keep a crew in any job more alert, observant, and engaged, minimizing mistakes and unnecessary double repairs.

We see the benefits of teamwork everywhere in life: professional sports, successful businesses, musical groups, emergency response teams, law firms, garbage truck crews, military outfits, and city councils, to name a few. Generally speaking, the reasons for assembling these teams are that (1) several people are better than one for sheer production, but more important, (2) fielding multiple players helps combine specialists in purposeful ways that yield better results overall.

Athletic coaches think about the second factor constantly. The number of players on a team is predetermined so their planning goes toward *how* to put those people in the right place at the right time for maximum effect. Who will play center on our basketball team and why? Who will play left wing on our soccer team and why? Which players might I switch if the game goes into overtime to give my field hockey team the edge they need? Coaches recognize through tryouts, practices, and games what the particular strengths of players are and how they might work together best. It is a major part of the job.

In the modern classroom, educational focus seems to be more and more individualized. We might see a group of thirty students in front of us not as a team, but as a loose conglomeration of separate entities. Perhaps we see them this way because we know that they will turn in assignments, take exams, receive grades, and sit for standardized tests individually. The educational system seems to favor isolated learning by virtue of the high priority placed on individual growth measures and reporting procedures.

Even so, we have a choice about how we see our students and how we train our team. We can determine how we will gather information about their strengths and weaknesses at the beginning of our allotted time with them—or perhaps beforehand—and throughout the course of instruction. We can keep tabs not only on how they are progressing individually but also interacting socially. We can observe and relish the unique, quirky, and wonderful traits that each of them brings to the table. We can pair and group them skillfully, noting how certain students seem to complement one another naturally. We can designate leaders, spokespersons, assistants, evaluators, discussants, observers, documenters, and presenters wisely, capitalizing on students' natural tendencies while also rotating those roles frequently.

We have the option of applying teamwork concepts to our classes if we are willing to break the mold of individual learning for individual testing. We can orchestrate fine-tuned human groups capable of accomplishing great tasks in creative and cooperative ways. We can rotate work responsibilities for projects and assignments to keep things fresh and broaden students' understanding. We can engage all students by matching them in unique ways to the smaller roles that together constitute the overarching activity. Better yet, students may start to approach tasks and challenges themselves this way if we have set the wheels in motion. In so many school situations, our students are all wearing the same number and playing the same position on the court with little interest in what each other is doing. Look for ways to field a real team in your classroom and let the whole outshine the parts.

KEY IDEAS:

- Choose a favorite example of effective teamwork and apply it to your students.
- Get to know your students even better and mastermind their roles for optimum growth.

ALL DAY WE ALTERNATE BETWEEN TEACHING AND LEARNING, AND SO DOES EVERYONE ELSE

Recognizing and reminding yourself of this can be a game changer in your career. We study and train so hard to become professional teachers, dedicating our lives to helping others learn day after day according to established guidelines and standards, and sometimes in very challenging environments. We are surrounded by a group of colleagues who have chosen the same and who carry out their work carefully, methodically, and conscientiously. This lifestyle can fool us into thinking that we are teachers and others are not, a sentiment that may be true in our professional occupation but downright silly in practical terms.

Perhaps sneakier, and possibly more dangerous, is that teaching students all day may lead us to believe occasionally that others are learners, and we are not. The truth is that everyone is a teacher and everyone is a learner at various points along the way in life. Ever learned something really valuable from a small child or even a baby? Someone older than you? More experienced? Less experienced? Someone who passed away hundreds of years ago? Someone you just met? Someone who did not even realize you were there? Ever taught something unexpectedly? Spontaneously? To a complete stranger? Perhaps to someone without your realizing it?

In my introductory course for music education majors, I assign a series of sequential tasks over a period of a couple of weeks. Students make mental or physical notes of the following situations they encounter outside of their classrooms:

- *learning something from others*
- *teaching something to others*
- *witnessing teaching in which they are not involved*
- *witnessing learning in which they are not involved*
- *learning from something besides humans*

Their discoveries, as you might guess, are always rather diverse and usually quite entertaining. They are pleased to report that they learned from and taught their roommates how to accomplish practical tasks that save time and money. They are proud to describe a professor or other "noted authority" around campus learning something from one of their buddies. They are often surprised to discover what they learn on a regular basis from inanimate objects, not only from obvious smartphones and tablets but also from revolving doors, city buses, noisy fluorescents, and sidewalks. They begin to understand—I think and hope—a much greater reciprocal relationship between teaching and learning, all of which informs their path toward "official" teaching.

Perhaps the most important results of these exercises are their conclusions about the roles of teacher and learner being shared among us all. Anytime we think of ourselves more as a teacher than a learner, we reduce the chance of picking up something new and valuable. We also likely reduce the chance of someone else, perhaps unexpectedly, rising up to teach something in the moment it is needed. Likewise, if we think of ourselves more as a learner than a teacher, we may miss the opportunity to offer something valuable to someone who really needs it. Let us carry on full steam ahead in both roles, and be sure to let others do the same.

KEY IDEAS:

- Teaching and learning naturally occur in a variety of ways for each of us.
- Seek constant balance between the two for your own and others' highest benefit.

TAKE IN INFORMATION ABOUT YOUR SCHOOL AND STUDENTS ON A NEED-TO-KNOW BASIS

This one is tough. We want to know as much about our school and students as possible when it is useful, but we also hear lots of things that are not conducive or relevant. Some of them are downright counterproductive and problematic, and unnecessarily so. There are things we wish we could "unhear" in the faculty lounge, at meetings, or from student conversations not intended for our ears.

If you agree that broad and deep knowledge of your school and students is crucial, but only when it is "your business," and you would prefer to leave extraneous information aside, consider your sources of school news and engage them wisely. The first and easiest decision to make, likely yielding the biggest results, is simply choosing when to ask for information and when to keep quiet. If a colleague has just described a big frustration with a particular student, keeping the account anonymous, don't ask who it was unless you really need to know. The answer might affect your relationship with that student, in perhaps an unjustified way. Maybe there was a misunderstanding or an honest mistake that you never hear about afterward, and you carry on with a falsely tainted image of that student's behavior patterns. In most cases, you can help and support your colleague without knowing who, specifically, was involved.

Another key factor in determining what sort of information you are likely to hear is choosing to whom you ask your questions. If, for instance, you want to know about a particular student's learning strengths and weaknesses to help her in class, but not also gossip about her personal life and extracurricular behaviors, you may have several choices among your colleagues who taught that student last year. Knowing those options, choose the teacher who will stick to the point, offer you information that will really contribute to the student's learning, and refrain from adding anything that might bias your view of her.

Finally, and usually more elusive, pay attention to situations in which a storm is developing by itself and be prepared to counteract it or evacuate. You may not have asked anyone anything, but find yourself in a conversation with students or colleagues that is quickly turning toward information you predict you do not want to know. You can feel it. You know the tide is turning in a way that simply won't help you help students any better tomorrow, and, in fact, might make it more difficult. If you have an opportunity to nip it in the bud, and steer the conversation back toward higher ground, do it. You might save everyone some trouble. If you can tell that there is no way that will work, excuse yourself from the conversation. You at least save yourself some time and energy and keep your focus in the right direction.

Staying current with information about our school and students helps us better serve their learning. We should share information freely and frequently, but only when it is beneficial. The line is all too easily crossed into negative gossip, personal problems, and irrelevant complaints or disputes. We also may encounter seemingly positive information that can have subtly inappropriate effects. For example, knowing that a certain student is your colleague's absolute favorite in the class or the daughter of a colleague's best friend can influence the way you treat him or her. See how fine the line is? You will be the one to judge what information is useful and pertinent, and what should be left alone. Pay attention to your radar and get in the habit of taking in information on a need-to-know basis.

KEY IDEAS:

- Gathering information about your students can be both helpful and problematic.
- Spend some time and energy experimenting with your need-to-know radar.

NOTICE LEARNING THAT IS HAPPENING
WITHOUT YOU, AND ENJOY IT

A few years ago, when my sons were rather young, I came home from campus expecting to engage in our daily greeting routine: I would rush in the back door, yelling and clapping, and the four of us would bounce around and bang into each other for a few minutes. That day, as I entered the house, volume and energy steadily rising, my oldest son (five years) lifted his hand very seriously and said quite calmly, "Wait, Dad. Matteo is learning to write his name." I stopped short and backed out of the living room without a peep, beaming the whole way. I had just witnessed a prime learning environment.

I'm an adult. A teacher. A parent. An educational researcher. An author. If anyone is well equipped to teach his youngest son how to write his name, it's me. Yet there is no way that I or anyone else could have created a better learning environment that day. All three children were intently focused, efficient, clear, and cooperative. It was palpable.

Perhaps this example can provide a light-hearted parallel for some of the situations we may encounter in the classroom. Even when the stakes are officially higher in an educational environment, and you are supposed to be the expert in the room with everything planned and prepared, you probably will find that some of the best learning happens when you are not involved. Yes, you might take credit for arranging the room, delivering the activity, or matching up pairs or groups of students, but they take it from there. In those moments, observe and enjoy. It is one of the secret perks we receive as part of the job.

Most likely one of the reasons you chose teaching is that you love to witness learning. Watching human beings grow and change, develop confidence in a certain subject, and take small steps and giant leaps forward is fascinating and rewarding work. Just because we are the paid professional in the room does not mean we need to control every movement; nor should we. One of the decisions wise teachers make frequently is to not interfere with learning that has been sparked spontaneously among students.

Several benefits arise from this decision. As in the opening example, peer interactions tend to generate an ideal learning pace and intrinsic motivation, especially when they are relatively spontaneous (read: "not micromanaged by you"). As we all know, teaching something usually helps us reinforce concepts more fully for ourselves, so the "teachers" in that moment are probably benefitting as much as the learners. Allowing learning to happen by itself also frees you to observe the entire room more carefully, perhaps helping you notice other needs. Finally, enjoying unexpected learning fosters a positive and proactive environment because you are sending out subtle signals like

"Learning is priority number one," "There are lots of ways to get there," and "You all have some pretty good ideas yourselves!"

Next time you are in class, be on the lookout for learning that does not involve you directly. Find a way to open up a bit of time and space to allow it to flourish fully. Give yourself the liberty to enjoy it internally at the very least, or perhaps even to crack a smile or acknowledge it aloud. These reactions might encourage a lot more of the same down the road.

KEY IDEAS:

- Quality learning may happen by itself spontaneously, especially if you make room for it.
- Part of our teacher role is deciding the difference between "helping" and "interfering."

IF STUDENTS DON'T HAVE A NEED TO LEARN SOMETHING, CREATE THAT NEED, OR DON'T TEACH IT

To create an ideal environment, students should feel the need to learn things. The proof of this shows up in everyday life all the time. When we really need to grasp the basic geography of a city we are visiting we will learn it, and fast. When we need to cook an unfamiliar recipe before family or friends arrive to dinner, we will soak up the information quickly. When we need to fix our car's automatic window or solve a plumbing problem in our house our absorption and assimilation skills shift into high gear. If, however, we are not in these situations our motivation and energy are not nearly as driven to study geography, recipes, electrical motors, or valve fittings.

When proactive people bump into a real need, solid learning follows. Conversely, without that need they may leave the learning alone. Students are people. They should be shown, or better yet, should discover for themselves *why* they need to learn certain things. Many subjects and topics in school are not as practically oriented as the examples above. Sometimes the reason to learn something in school is simply to develop a more fully functioning mind, capable of transferring information across situations and discovering what is necessary to solve problems in that discipline and others. If so, students should be made clearly aware of that. If students think they are learning something because teachers think it is wonderful or important, but they see no reason for it themselves, they will be led to believe they are learning it for our sake. Our job is to help them see why it is important for *them*, and a bit of explanation can go a long way.

Perhaps even more useful than an explanation is the invention of a situation that helps students realize the need for themselves. If basic geography skills are the goal, perhaps a short field trip would provide the impetus. If understanding and executing detailed recipes is the plan, then a bake sale by the Health and Nutrition class might be in order. If common electrical motors and valve fittings are the focus, we might assign students to survey their adult family members to discover what problems they have had with their own cars and residences, and what the associated costs or personal labor investment was. These sorts of forays can help students see why a given topic actually matters, generating a true need rather than a secondary desire like high grades or praise. The added benefit of this approach is that students start to see school as a place that is actually there to help them, not just to put them to work—and especially not to put them to work for poor reasons.

Let us assume you are very passionate about your subject, and you have made your curricular decisions with the students' absolute best interests in mind. *You* know why they need to learn the things you have selected, but *they* may not realize it, at least not clearly enough. Make it explicit. Appeal to them in ways you know will catch their attention. Be creative about how you show them why each topic is worth their time.

Finally, if students are not interested in learning something, and if you really cannot create a need for it, consider not teaching it. Is it really that important? Is there some other reason you are teaching it, such as the fact that it was taught to you, or that experts seem to agree it is important, or that students ought to endure some hard work to "build character"? Sometimes we deceive ourselves into thinking we have a good reason to teach something, but the student need is not actually there . . . and cannot even be contrived. Ask yourself these tough questions before students do. It may help you trim down your lesson plans to those topics and skills that truly address students' needs, leaving you extra time and energy to approach them in authentic ways.

KEY IDEAS:

- Communicate clearly with students regarding your reasons for curricular content.
- Help students discover how their learning applies before and as they engage in it.

THE CLEARER YOUR COMMAND OF THE BIG PICTURE, THE BETTER YOU CAN DELIVER THE CHALLENGES

A few years ago, I had the opportunity to offer some spontaneous and surreptitious soccer coaching to my sons and three of their friends. What began as a trip to the park with a lot of sports equipment and no plan soon turned into a 3-v-3 soccer match with me playing defense for both sides. I was honored just to be invited to play; little did I know I would learn a thing or two about teaching that day.

All the boys were between 8 and 10 years old, so I had the physical advantage by far. I also have played soccer all my life so I could see the plays unfolding and could take control of a given moment when necessary. I quickly found myself "teaching" a litany of individual skills, principles of teamwork, and field awareness without any of the boys (and sometimes even me) knowing it.

For instance, one particular player tended not to pass. Ever. I crowded him relentlessly and he gradually realized he could not keep that up. His passing improved dramatically. Others tended to just swat at the ball without really collecting it with their feet. I gave them a little extra room and guarded their teammates so they learned to take an extra second, get the ball under control, and look at their options. Some players tried to sneak closer and closer to the goal for a point-blank shot, so I would rush them early and steal the ball. They learned to take a shot right away when they had the chance. And on and on.

The point of these examples is that I was in a position to influence the environment such that the boys were bound to learn valuable lessons. I certainly did not let on that I would be coaching them that day; in fact, I didn't even talk about any of the things I was doing. Not even a "See, you have to learn to pass." I simply did what was needed to prompt them to make the leaps forward themselves.

Think of all the talking, nagging, and convincing those brief episodes may have replaced.

How might this dynamic apply to classroom teaching? Are there student actions you can influence in subtle yet powerful ways through your vision of the big picture and ability to play numerous roles in learning interactions? Are you using your expertise to the fullest in every class? Do you find yourself verbally reminding students of some things over and over? Is there some other way to make those points "hit home" right away? Are there aspects of students' learning that could be more efficient, more applicable, or more realistic?

The beauty of a classful of students is the combination of a great number of moving parts. We see individuals moving in certain directions, both physically and mentally, throughout the day. We may have more options than we realize for how we can assist them in directing and redirecting their focus and subsequent moves. If you picture a soccer coach, you might imagine someone yelling from the sidelines or literally drawing up plays to illustrate what the team needs to do. Coaching, though, can also take the form of running around on the field among the players during practice, spontaneously making their lives reasonably difficult until they learn to play smarter and better. Likewise, if you picture a teacher, you might imagine someone lecturing at the front of the room or demonstrating an operation. Teaching, though, can also take many forms, some of which can and should be equally spontaneous and surreptitious. Seek out your true role in every class every day and play it well.

KEY IDEAS:

- The better and broader your skills set, the greater your effectiveness as a teacher.
- Teaching can take a variety of formats; choose the most direct for a given situation.

HIGH STUDENT ENGAGEMENT DOES NOT IMPLY THAT ALL STUDENTS ARE DOING THE SAME THING

In fact, it's usually quite the contrary. Every group of students reflects some degree of diversity in background knowledge, motivation, and creativity, for example, and sometimes quite a bit. "Engaging the class" means engaging that diversity even if on the surface it appears that everyone is attending to a common overarching goal.

That common goal should not be understated, of course. It is important, in most cases, to establish a clear trajectory, a general direction in which all students are moving together. This helps build momentum in the room, generates collective experience, and greases the wheels of collaboration. Within that large wave, though, are lots of smaller ripples created by the particular needs of individuals and the moves they must make to face their unique challenges. Teachers can help by identifying targeted areas of growth for individuals, or at least small groups, and seeking creative ways to engage them in that work.

A great deal of customized student engagement can be accomplished simply through *choices*. Teachers work awfully hard between class meetings to evaluate students' work, provide feedback, and prepare for the next round. It can be tempting to have everyone do the exact same thing for each learning activity—easier to grade and better for keeping everyone parallel. However, broadening the possibilities and opening up options for students may be more beneficial to them and even surprisingly helpful to you.

For example, do all students need to write a reflection on the same book, article, poem, or short story or could they each pick one that grabs their attention? Do they all have to complete the same three physical strength and endurance tests for their quarterly grade or could they choose two and you choose one from a list? Do all students have to engineer the same toothpick structure or could they determine their choice from their daily travels out there in the real world? Do all students need to do the even numbered math problems tonight or could they choose even or odd? Or select any three problems from each section? Or create their own problems reflecting the content of the evens? The possibilities go on and on.

Even in activities with some degree of choice built in, is there room for more? Creating that space might just light students' fires. Do all students need to satisfy the same grading criteria for the science fair project they chose or could they stretch and bend the categories for optimally effective reporting? Must everyone produce their creative writing journal, musical composition, or family tree using the same software program and guidelines or are there possibilities for innovative presentation and accompanying inspiration?

The thought of introducing choices like these into students' activities may seem initially overwhelming. Where will we find the time and energy to manage that diversity and evaluate such a breadth of submitted work? Too much choice is too much choice, and we certainly should avoid overdoing it. However, maintaining a diversity of engagement through these sorts of options can actually be helpful to us too. We may find that students' work encourages us to keep learning, to stay open to content and to ways of presenting it that we may not have yet explored. We might discover a rejuvenating freshness in a pile of book reports, grandparent interviews, article analyses, or still life paintings that simply would not be there if we kept everyone strictly in line. Suddenly, grading all that work might *give* you a rush of energy rather than slowly depleting it.

KEY IDEAS:

- Look for opportunities to introduce more student choice into activities and assignments.
- Helping students stay engaged in their own best ways can help you stay engaged in yours.

WHENEVER POSSIBLE, CHOOSE THE RIPEST LEARNING OPPORTUNITY AT THAT MOMENT

We tend to use the word "ripe" most frequently to refer to fruits and vegetables, though it can be appropriate for grains, wine, cheese, age, and even opportunities. The ripest apple on the tree is the one most ready to pick. It might not be the closest or easiest—in fact, it usually isn't, is it? —but it is the one most worthwhile to harvest at that moment. The others that are closer, more convenient, and more abundant still need to mature a bit.

Learning opportunities follow a similar path: not only *learning* in general but also learning *opportunities*, those moments that seem to well up unexpectedly, sometimes presenting themselves with accompanying trumpet fanfare and at other times in a silent, almost secretive way. Teachers must be masters of spotting the ripest fruit and, more important, of finding the flexibility in the moment to help students pick it.

If that perfect proverbial apple is hanging far out on a high branch, we might need a large ladder, a special tool, or a friend to help us get it. We might actually climb through lots of other apples on our way to it. We might need extra time and effort, and even put ourselves in uncomfortable positions, because that piece of fruit has been prepared just right. Convenience takes a backseat to quality.

One of the traps that student teachers often fall into the most is sticking to their plan no matter what. They may even realize it themselves, but after the fact. Fine-tuning the balance between prior plan and present perception is a career-long quest. We may pass milestones along the way, in which we discover certain indicators that help us make decisions, but the process is an organic one that shifts gradually and constantly depending on learning circumstances.

One factor that can help us strike that balance effectively is paying close attention to all learning opportunities that present themselves in a given moment. If you have pondered several key points that need to be addressed prior to class, you will be more likely to notice them if they show up in a spontaneous, timely, yet unexpected, fashion. In other words, in your lesson planning take the time to consider what additional topics are related to tomorrow's focus, what concepts will likely follow it next week, and what may be some seemingly unrelated concepts that you might be *always* ready to entertain.

The ripest apple is usually the easiest one to actually pick, once you find yourself in reach of it. In fact, if you left it there another week it might fall of its own accord, but could be full of worms or half-rotten, or get swiped by a rabbit or squirrel. You have to pluck it from the tree at just the right moment, and it will show you when the time is right if you are watching. Similarly, students will provide the best indicators of the best learning opportunities. Listen carefully to their questions, comments, and perhaps confusions not only attempting to solve them as definitively and efficiently as possible but also thinking about how those queries might instead lend themselves to a related, more substantial opportunity. The smaller, bitter apples hanging right at eye level often clue us in to the delicious fruit tucked in just a few branches away.

KEY IDEAS:

- Some of the best learning opportunities are a bit harder to find. Keep looking.
- The best indicators of a rising opportunity usually come directly from students.

BE WILLING TO LET STUDENTS MAKE A MISTAKE; IN FACT, EMBRACE IT WITH GRATITUDE

Mistakes generally carry a negative connotation. We avoid them, regret them, and correct them. We remember our mistakes to make sure we do not repeat them. We even pass along our mistake stories to others, hoping to spare them the same trouble in the future. Mistakes can be costly in terms of finances, health, or reputation of an individual or organization. We generally lose something, to some extent, when we make them, except in education.

What a fascinating thing formal learning really is. Meant to reflect the "real world," but in a relatively vague sense. Education means people growing on purpose, with a commitment to broad scope and swift pace, centered on noticeable change in those young hearts and minds. In school, everything serves the goal of students' being better today than they were yesterday.

Enter mistakes. We might see them in school in two categories, those that are relatively harmless, quickly contributing to student growth in obvious ways, and those that are grave errors carrying truly negative consequences. The truth though, which can be hard to accept in the heat of the moment, is that all mistakes in school can be used for student growth. Outcomes depend on teachers' and students' breadth of perspective, commitment to improvement, and creativity.

For example, a student may miss a detail in a reading passage resulting in an incorrect answer on the quiz. This is a simple mistake with relatively mild consequences that could teach a lesson like "Always go back and check your answer carefully against the relevant spot in the text." Lesson learned; future tasks improved. On the other hand, a student might study all the wrong material for a major literature test and bomb it. Big red *F*. This mistake may be harder to handle, perhaps generating embarrassment, a lower term grade, or loss of honor roll status.

Similarly, a math student might miss a small step in a word problem (easy to accept and improve) or apply the wrong memorized equation for a whole series of items on the Scholastic Aptitude Test (harder to bear). A physical education student might mistakenly aim the tennis ball at the wrong part of the court, resulting in a lost point (easy to accept and improve), or fail to maintain awareness of her court position, resulting in a broken racquet and nose (harder to bear).

In each of these contrasting pairs, the milder mistake is easier to embrace and squeeze for its educational opportunities. The heavier mistakes are harder to accept because of the consequences they bring, but can be all the more powerful in the lessons they teach. We don't like to see our students fail, but fail they must for their own good. Far better to mess things up in school under our guidance and with the main goal of moving on and getting better than to make their mistakes later in life when they are expected to be already finished and polished. Furthermore, learning how to use mistakes, one's own and others', for positive change is one of the most important and far-reaching lessons people can learn as students. Teachers must be rather wise about how they treat mistakes if students are to learn to handle them well.

These examples are probably easy to digest in their broad and distant terms, but mistakes that *your* students are making right now in *your* classrooms may be harder to accept. Remember that mistakes can be every bit as good as, and sometimes better than, pre-planned, well-oiled, perfectly executed tasks. It really does help to see what happens when something doesn't work as it should. Keep guiding your students to avoid truly dangerous or catastrophic errors, but be willing to let them make lots of reasonable and helpful ones. In fact, embrace those with gratitude. Chances are your students will learn to do the same.

KEY IDEAS:

- Mistakes can be difficult to accept in the moment, but valuable down the road.
- School is for constructing student learning, and mistakes are a great tool.

"CORRECT" ANSWERS ARE USEFUL ONLY FOR EVENTUALLY SURPASSING THEM

Think about it. For a submitted answer to be correct, it must be compared to some preexisting template answer. The information has already been processed, distilled, and formatted into a recognizable truth within our subject matter. The students' job is to reprocess, redistill, and reformat the information to come up with the same result, proving their mastery of the material. This could take place in an informal, spontaneous discussion in class or on a high-stakes exam. It could show up as a multiple-choice item, a lengthy essay, or a complicated skills demonstration. In all cases, the correct answer is already old news.

Did the students spell the list of words correctly? Solve the equation properly (showing their work, of course)? Organize the timeline in proper order? Play the melody with the right rhythm? Describe three results of the Industrial Revolution fully and accurately? Use the right number of syllables in their haiku?

We can see how these questions may reflect important milestones in students' understanding and skills development, but they also reflect knowledge that has been around for quite a while. Each may also reflect a task that groups of students in your class have demonstrated year after year in almost identical fashion. There's nothing wrong with that; a good test is a good test.

However, demonstrating the correct answers in all of these cases really should serve as a springboard for exploring new territory. Students need to be urged to think about the material in ways that haven't been thought before—ways that do not yet yield correct and incorrect answers but, for now, "correct-neutral" results. That is, can you offer students prompts, questions, and challenges for which you do not have a prepared answer, perhaps not even a sketch of one in mind? Are you willing to accompany and guide students through the sort of thinking that professionals do in the field, rather than sticking to what is already known for sure, and easy to evaluate?

Correct answers are certainly important for growth. They help us sequence learning, check understanding, build confidence and momentum, and avoid reinventing the wheel. Beware the tangible satisfaction and convenient efficiency they provide, though. The other edge of that sword is complacency and conformity. If students are striving to produce only correct answers, they are striving only to catch up with old knowledge. Though it may seem scary at first, try developing a few prompts for concepts or activities for which there is no correct answer or right way, at least not yet.

Strangely enough, we encounter lots of situations in daily life for which there is no correct answer, or in which the "correct" answer can be negotiated, or in which it can change automatically according to environmental factors or passing time. Yet, in education we seem to focus unduly on planned content that is designed ultimately to check whether students can match predetermined benchmarks. While this approach can help us focus our time with students and keep them on track, it doesn't necessarily provide much inspiration or true motivation. Consider the possibility that correct answers are useful only for eventually surpassing them, and watch how far students go.

KEY IDEAS:

- Correct answers are a valuable part of education, but may provide limited potential.
- Seek a healthy balance between correct-answer content and exploratory material.

NOTHING STAYS THE SAME, INCLUDING EDUCATION

Witnessing change is so easy. Grass grows. Pipes rust. Babies are born. Seniors graduate. Winter comes. Breakfast is over. Opportunities arrive. Friends leave town. In fact, change is constant—in education, too. The question for teachers is how we engage it; that is, how our approach reflects the change already happening in our students and learning environments.

The challenge in education is that a large part of our job is passing along what is known. By its nature, teaching involves some amount of dwelling in the past. Even if we are bringing students the latest developments in our field regularly, that "new" information is already at least a little bit old. We are called to present students with time-tested truths in a constantly changing world. The temptation is to lean too far in one of two directions, either ignoring change and clinging stubbornly to the way things have always been, or embracing change completely and throwing out any sense of stability and organization within our content area.

Ideally, we must reconcile the two, clarifying and stabilizing the essential body of knowledge and skills we pass on to students while also adapting our pedagogical approach to the inevitable change we see in them and their environment. It is not uncommon for us to catch ourselves simply teaching how we were taught, but sometimes inappropriately so. For example, we may present a concept or deliver a lecture or presentation much like our teachers did when we were in school, even when we know there is a better way. Or perhaps we require students to take notes a certain way or submit assignments according to given parameters that may be far outdated.

To say that "education" needs to keep changing mostly means that teachers need to keep changing. We must adapt the resources we use, the ways we communicate, the rules we maintain, the priorities we publish, the expectations we have, and the content we choose. Sometimes this change comes about in big bursts, prompted by federal legislation, standardized testing, school district policy, or administrative decisions. A whole course or curriculum might be completely revamped and rewritten to keep up with the times. At other times, change can happen quite gradually and seamlessly, prompted directly by teachers. This second option may reflect the constant change in our world more truthfully, occurring bit by bit as needs arise.

We vary widely in our relationships to change. Some teachers are quite set in their ways, apparently not even desiring to shift. Others seem never to be the slightest bit satisfied, constantly switching and reorganizing even to the detriment of students' learning. Explore your relationship to change in education, not "capital E" education that we read about in the news, but the education happening right there in your own classroom. Do you carefully observe the shifts you are seeing in your students and your school culture? Can you make slight adjustments on a regular basis that will enhance students' learning by connecting with them on today's terms? Can you honor the crucial content in your field fully while maintaining relevance to current conditions? Can you use the pedagogy of the past as a point of departure rather than a static template?

A final factor to consider is that *you* are also changing. Teachers sometimes entertain the thought that our students are moving on, that our field is evolving, that our schools are growing and transforming, and even our colleagues are changing, but that we are the central hub around which it all revolves. We teachers not only should pride ourselves on our consistency and dependability but also recognize that we change personally over the course of a career. We need to come to terms with that early and frequently so that we can make the most of it as we adapt our teaching style. Perhaps the most fundamental mistake we can make in the classroom is not being our genuine selves. Students sniff it out immediately and it does no one any good. Paying close attention to ways your own life is unfolding can have a profound impact on how you approach students, keeping your relationship with them up-to-date at all times.

The sheer number of factors contributing to change in education can be daunting. We are called to teach tried-and-true material in cutting-edge ways. Our schools and student populations undergo both minor and major transformations on a regular basis. We ourselves are changing as we reconcile all of these inputs to make them work for students. The tendency may be to hunker down and stick with what we know, what is safe, what worked last year, what worked a generation ago. This simply won't do though—it can't do, because the world has moved on. Don't wait for "education" to change; it is waiting for you.

KEY IDEAS:

- Educational change need not be a huge shift; find little ways that make a big difference.
- Keep an eye on your own changing self; be honest and stay genuine with your students.

THE BEST APPROACH TO SUCCESSFUL CLASSROOM MANAGEMENT IS BEING IN THE RIGHT JOB

Classroom management may be the longest-running "hot topic" in teacher training history; the focus of conversations in faculty lounges; the title of so many in-service presentations; and the stuff of educational textbooks and recertification courses. More tangibly, the legitimate concern of many teachers, and perhaps the main reason some of them question their choice of profession or even leave it.

The title above may sound naïve. "Well, sure, if I had my ideal job, classroom management would be a cinch." "If I had *those* students instead of *these* students, I'm sure everything would be smoother." "If I worked at *that* school with *those* administrators, life would be great in class." If you have entertained these thoughts, but not deeply investigated them, now is the time. What is it about *those* students or *that* environment that you think would make everything okay? What, exactly, does your ideal job look like? What are the key components that would make it so? What are your "must-haves" for a satisfactory work environment? And how does all of this affect classroom management?

Putting the right teacher in the right classroom is essential for its full functioning. Obvious evidence for this would be placing a top-notch teacher in one subject into a classroom of another and watching things quickly deteriorate. The "famous" biology teacher would probably not fare so well in French class, nor vice versa. Sure, some people are just plain good at maintaining students' focus and keeping them in line, but that by itself is more like crowd control than classroom management.

Great classroom management entails total integration, where all the moving parts are working together relatively smoothly and seamlessly toward essential common goals. The right students and the right teacher in the right place at the right time would be ideal to make this happen. We should certainly strive toward that ideal description, and the component we can control the most is providing the right teacher.

What material do you *really* want to teach? How do you want the daily "action" of your class to look? How do you envision your students? What would be your ideal relationship with them? What sort of colleagues and administrators would inspire you regularly and make you want to inspire them back? These questions can be useful for both pre-service teachers engaged in the job search and seasoned teachers with an established position. Answering them poses at least three possibilities: (1) seek a different (or first) job in which your contributions will be highly conducive to student success; (2) make substantial changes in your current position to match what you envision as a fully functioning classroom; or (3)—and this is the hard one—determine whether perhaps you are already in the right job but are not meeting it appropriately as it is.

There are two sides to this equation: "the job" and you. External factors can be sought, chosen, and changed. So can internal ones. For those of you seeking your first job, weigh all of these factors carefully and honestly. Push yourself to imagine your best job vividly and go after it. For those already teaching, if you experience classroom management issues regularly take a good look at these reflective questions to see if you are in the right job. If not, determine what to do about it and *make those changes*. Finally, if you have very few classroom management issues, count your blessings, identify what is working for you, and by all means, pass it along.

KEY IDEAS:

- Classroom management issues are usually not the problem, but the symptom.
- You may have more options than you realize for improving the "job-you" relationship.

NEVER TEACH THE SAME CLASS TWICE

Although this is stated like a suggestion, it really is a given. Just as you cannot step into the same proverbial river twice because it is in constant flow, you cannot teach the same class twice because all factors, especially students, are different each time. Simple enough—case closed, right? The problem is that we still try.

Whether it is two or more sections of a course meeting during one day or one week, or a repeated course from marking period to marking period or school year to school year, we not only reap the benefits but also risk the drawbacks of repeating a teaching experience. Conscientious reflection on previous iterations of a class can improve our instruction dramatically. It helps us fine-tune our pacing, decide whether to keep or discard examples, and strengthen the relationship between learning and assessment, all within the helpful context of 20/20 hindsight. Teachers often quip that their second period class is so lucky to get a better teacher every day because of what they tweaked after first period, or that this year's students are in such better shape than last year's because the teacher has made significant changes.

Recognizing potential improvements and making them swiftly is one benefit to teaching a class multiple times; realizing what already worked splendidly and keeping it is another. We may explore a metaphor in class spontaneously to respond to a student's question and later identify it as a "keeper" for the future. Perhaps we discover that a certain sequence of activities maintained student engagement surprisingly well and note it in our lesson plan for next time around.

We may also keep things parallel across multiple sections of a class just for consistency. We want to make sure that students in both Period 1 and Period 2 are confident about the core concepts we targeted in a given week, or that this year's students are equally well prepared to move up a grade as last year's students. Maintaining consistency across daily interactions and activities helps us keep everything organized and everyone on the same page. This is often more of a necessity than a luxury.

The trouble with teaching the same class twice comes when we try to do it too precisely. That is, we try to step into that same river a second time even though we know yesterday's water is long gone. We try out the same funny story or riveting example only to discover that it doesn't resonate at all with the students currently in front of us. We try to plan into the discussion a worthwhile tangent that arose organically during first period, only to find that it goes nowhere in second period. Somehow students were not drawn in like before and it fell flat. Naturally, these are not the same students.

There is a fine line between maintaining consistency across parallel classes and trying to actually teach the same class twice. To keep things fresh and genuine, we have to harness the tools and approaches we have used before, and target the same big ideas and skills, but all the while attentively teaching the students that sit before us in the present moment. During standard roll call, when students respond "here," we hope that they are really "here" in every way that day. Make sure that you and your lesson plan are really "here" every time too, especially when you are teaching a given class again or . . . . *AGAIN.* Never teach the same class twice.

KEY IDEAS:

- A fine line exists between maintaining class consistency and recreating it exactly.
- Keen awareness in the moment helps us reconcile repeated content and new students.

DON'T TEACH THE WAY SOMEONE ELSE THINKS IS BEST

Sure, this might happen coincidentally sometimes, but what is implied here is that we cannot afford to go against our own knowledge of how best to reach our students due to someone else's recommendations. Pre-service teachers face this challenge all too often. They try to apply someone else's opening activity, skill demonstration, or classroom management tactic only to see it fail miserably. Why? Because they were trying too hard to emulate someone else rather than making the material their own. What's more, they *knew* they were doing it but decided to recreate the recipe rather than respond to the reality.

Trusting one's own instincts and adapting class plans quickly and appropriately generally improves with experience. More important, one's confidence (and perhaps freedom) to do so runs a similar course. Throughout our careers most teachers meet mentors, official and unofficial, from student-teaching cooperating teachers to early-career mentor colleagues to retiring predecessors passing the torch. These people have valuable insights to offer, some of which may be rather prescriptive and seemingly set in stone. Absorbing their help is very important, but so is using it in ways that align with our own teaching philosophy and style.

Several considerations may help point the way. First, no matter how stern or forceful the advice or suggestions, mentors' input is usually meant to be genuinely helpful. Perspectives, strategies, and daily activities put forth by college professors, textbook authors, bloggers, and teaching mentors are offered to save you time and trouble. Many of these contributors will clearly remind you to take what they give and make it your own. Others may not. You must take that next step yourself to ensure you are using their input wisely and appropriately. Deep down, all contributors would expect you to do so, no matter how enamored they may seem to be with their own ideas as stated.

Second, just because you agree wholeheartedly with someone else's overarching philosophy or approach does not mean you have to stick to it in all cases for all time. Remember that they may not even have done so themselves! Again, whether they state it openly or not, all of those mentoring voices would probably hope that you would make exceptions and adaptations where better student growth may be possible.

Finally, beware of the perceived strength of particular personalities and experts. Gauge the merit of mentors' contributions honestly and rigorously, and don't accept anything for your students that you are not completely convinced is worth their while. Just because an influential voice speaks loudly or powerfully does not mean it is completely correct or better than the others.

We probably listen to those louder voices a bit too often, simply because they draw our attention more quickly and fully. Learn to hear them equally with the other voices involved, including your own, and to tune them out when appropriate.

This is not to suggest that you already know all you need to know or that you should always just follow your gut. Others have many valuable things to offer you. Accept them graciously. However, those others will not be performing your job with your students tomorrow morning, so be prepared to adapt what they have given you in shrewdly and meticulously prepared ways for the unique group you know and love. Honor others' input fully by incorporating it in ways you know will help your students the most. Don't just teach the way someone else thinks is best.

KEY IDEAS:

- Mentors can be a great help, but it is our responsibility to make their guidance our own.
- Pay plenty of attention to the quieter voices, including your own, for students' benefit.

TIMING IS EVERYTHING—IN TEACHING TOO

As the old joke goes, "Timing is . . . everything." Unfortunately, that is how things sometimes happen in our lives and classrooms. Things occur just a little too early or late and opportunities either vanish or become more difficult than they should be. Some of these timing situations are totally, or mostly, out of our control. Others are totally, or mostly, dependent on our decision-making in the moment. Your timing as a teacher is certainly a flexible skill, requiring you to be highly attentive and responsive to your environment and students.

The interesting thing about timing is that both speeding up and slowing down the next step in a learning sequence generally require quickness from you. Obviously, our decision to move something along usually has to come fast. We may be deep into an interaction with students and realize that they are ready to proceed or that now would be the perfect time to detour into a related topic. The idea must come to us and we must act on it rather swiftly to maintain the momentum in the room. However, the opposite is also true. Deliberately choosing to delay or prolong the timing of an explanation, demonstration, prompt, or response also requires quick recognition and swift decision-making on the spot.

Timing, of course, is intricately linked with sequencing. Much of our job description involves deciding what to do with students, in what order, and for how long. The first part, what to do, is usually already determined. It may be laid out in education standards, district curriculum, or individual lesson plans. The sequence in which we guide students through mastery of that material is also mostly obvious. Understanding what fractions actually are precedes sub-tracting or multiplying them, identifying verbs precedes identifying adverbs, and learning a solid forehand precedes polishing a drop shot. Some of these and other examples can be debated, but the fact remains that many learning sequences just make sense, so much so that they can be collaboratively final-ized in document form during curriculum development.

Timing, on the other hand, usually requires much more awareness and flexibility. We can build timing estimates into our lesson plans but they will likely shift, much more so than content or sequencing. The potential frustra-tion with—and sheer beauty of—timing is that it is constantly changing. We cannot afford to think of timing in the classroom as something that remains solely under our purview—not if we are doing things well. Rather, timing must be recognized as something that happens collectively, in macro- and micro-versions, and that must be adapted as constantly as possible to keep things running smoothly.

If we look at nature we see timing at its best. The seasons come and go, the weather changes, and the flora and fauna respond, but not at exactly the same time every year. The content and sequence mostly stay intact, changing a bit from year to year or over many years, but the timing is consistently inconsistent. Plants and animals seem to adapt effortlessly to these shifts, while humans are probably the last to surrender. We bemoan the summer heat wave that "just shouldn't be" or the winter that keeps "hanging on" past its due date. If, however, we decide to take a defiant stance and start wearing short-sleeve shirts before winter has finished, we'll be in for an unpleasant surprise. We must adapt to the greater timing that is happening around us and calibrate our own to it. The same goes in the classroom.

The trouble with these last two statements is that it would seem to detract from our authority. Are we to simply "let class happen" without attending to the time allotted and the goals we have set? Can we afford to allow students' (sometimes terrible) timing to overshadow our own well-laid plans? These are questions worth pursuing honestly. If we give up all ownership of timing in class, we and our students will probably meet chaos pretty quickly. However, if we learn to notice the timing that is already happening all around us and seek consistently to fuse it with the timing we intended or predicted, we may find that the two-way street functions beautifully.

A great way to experiment with your relationship to time is outside of class in your own life, in relatively low-stakes situations. Start by simply noticing the timing of things: light traffic, heavy traffic, no traffic, long lines, short conversations, fast transactions, and the "perfect" movie length. What sorts of factors contribute to the good or poor timing in these events? In what ways do people cause that timing and feel its effects? What relationship do you have to the timing of these moments? How can you influence them, or influence yourself internally as you experience them? Can you pinpoint or estimate what would be, or would have been, the ideal timing in a given situation?

The more you pay attention to timing throughout your day, the more focus you likely will place on it in the classroom. Finding yourself frustrated by examples of poor timing in "regular life" can be a great inspiration for striving to influence timing in the classroom as conscientiously as possible. Likewise, discovering timing that works splendidly in regular life can provide valuable insights into how you might apply it to that same classroom.

Content established? Check.
Sequence planned? Check.
Timing? TBD . . .

KEY IDEAS:

- Timing can be delicate and fickle; it is worth our full attention in the classroom.
- Examples of good and bad timing abound in life; use them to your teaching advantage.

IT'S OKAY FOR THINGS TO GO WELL

Pre-service teachers in college education courses practice a lot in front of their peers, trying out a lesson plan, leading an activity to apply a recently learned approach, and just getting up in front of people again and again to build confidence in their academic leadership skills. The instructor and peers may naturally find many things to fix; that is part of the learning process. In fact, college education majors often have to be reminded to reinforce something positive they saw or heard in the teacher's lesson because they become so intent on identifying and fixing the areas that need improvement.

Once in a while, though, a sample lesson simply goes splendidly. On a recent such occasion in my capstone course, I opened the floor for peer comments and the students were actually struggling to find something to offer for improvement. They said things like "That was really great; gosh, I'm trying to think of something for constructive criticism . . ." Even the peer teacher was asking "Could I have done this; should I have done that?" also seemingly searching for something that could or should be changed. There was a strange sense of urgency in the room to conjure up something negative and I found myself blurting out with a chuckle, "You know, it's okay for things to go well."

We all had a good laugh in the moment, and launched into a short discussion of the need to acknowledge those relatively rare moments when everything runs really smoothly and works out perfectly fine. We teachers are careful to not look at things through rose-colored glasses, and we take very seriously our responsibility to seek and destroy misunderstandings and learning obstacles on a daily basis. Yet sometimes things simply go well and we should be ready to highlight that for the good of our students and ourselves.

These acknowledgments are a form of positive reinforcement and can produce striking results. Not only does everyone in the room feel good about what just happened, but everyone comes to understand the event as an example of what the group is striving to achieve consistently. For instance, you might predict that today's activity will leave a handful of students behind, and that you will need to assign additional tasks to the other students while you help the strugglers. To your surprise, all students finish the task approximately at the same time because various pairs and small groups spontaneously rallied around each other to keep everyone on track. You don't know why this miracle suddenly happened, without your intervention, but you do know that you have the opportunity to make a public point of it. Doing so can boost positive energy across the room while also subtly suggesting that tomorrow's class might follow suit.

Teachers are full-time problem-solvers. We face lots of challenges and obstacles ourselves, all while guiding large groups of others through the same. We get easily accustomed to working in battle mode, scanning for trouble and pushing past it. If we don't stop to enjoy when things go well, though, we are being a bit dishonest. Accepting and acknowledging a balance of failures and successes is a lifelong lesson we have the opportunity to teach. Yes, part of our job is to pinpoint what needs to be fixed, but it's okay for things to go well too.

KEY IDEAS:

- Be willing to admit when things go splendidly well.
- Students can learn a lot from mistakes *and* successes, both others' and their own.

Chapter 2

Your Students

FIND YOUR FASCINATION WITH HUMAN BEINGS

On a recent sunny afternoon, I stopped for a short break in a small urban park in Philadelphia. I sat on a bench with no particular intentions. As people strode by, this way and that, I noted more than a few basic descriptors: tall, short, fast, slow, friendly, distant, arguing, reacting, encouraging, telling, watching, listening, tired, driven, relaxed, energetic, speaking other languages, not speaking at all, "speaking" with expressions and gestures, big, small, young, old, focused, scattered, patient, irritable, warm. All this within a minute or two at most. The trees, squirrels, birds, blue sky, and gently falling leaves were all there in their splendor, and the cars and buses vied for my attention too. But the people . . . oh, those fascinating human beings!

If we have embraced the age-old notion that we are not teaching a given school subject, but teaching people, we would do well to find our fascination with humans. One can assume that teachers have a high level of general interest in human being and development, but what is it particularly that intrigues you about people? Not necessarily what you like about them, or what you expect of them, or how you relate to them, or what you know, intellectually, about them. It may include any or all of those things, but what is it, exactly, that makes humans so *interesting* to you?

Asking yourself this question frequently and deeply can yield some surprises, because you may find that both "good" and "bad" human traits and tendencies show up in your answers. For instance, you may be impressed by the capacity people have to sympathize with one another and lend a helping hand but also genuinely intrigued by the way that criminal minds work. You may discover that you have always internally celebrated those warm moments of cooperation and collaboration you witness among family, friends, or perfect strangers, while also admiring the fierce independence and cold, hard focus of certain individuals. These contrasts highlight the wide diversity of the human condition. We are complex beings who not only exhibit diverse personality traits but also may change them in an instant according to our environment. When this potentially overwhelming picture presents itself as a class of students before you, be prepared to exercise your fascination with human beings.

From the teacher's perspective, humans should be tops on our list of what is most interesting in this world. The fact that everything taught and learned in the classroom is filtered through people is a crucial underpinning of classroom dynamics; ironically, we tend to forget that sometimes. We may lose sight of the actual people in front of us as we tackle a concept, treating it as if it existed by itself and momentarily forgetting that there is no learning without humans. There is nothing interesting without humans to make it so. There is no progress without humans to chart it. There is nothing worthwhile to discuss, debate, accept, dismiss, assimilate, evaluate, or test without humans doing it.

School is for people. The trees, squirrels, birds, blue sky, and gently falling leaves don't care about school. The school building doesn't care about school. The digital projector, desk, and textbook don't care about school. School is about people teaching and people learning. Let us first learn people. Find your fascination with human beings.

KEY IDEAS:

- All the important stuff in a classroom happens through people.
- Lifelong curiosity about human being is top priority for teachers.

NEVER SURRENDER YOUR VISION OF STUDENTS' TRUE GROWTH

Students' responses, contributions, and achievements are rarely *exactly* what we expect them to be. They constantly surprise us with how quickly or slowly they proceed and results may vary. Teachers' expectations for students vary too. Some teachers seem always to hold very high hopes for class outcomes, demanding much and pushing students hard to the very end. Rarely, if ever, are they satisfied. Others take a more relaxed stance, maintaining open space and appealing to students' natural pace. They may be satisfied all too easily. Most of us probably fall somewhere in the middle of that range. No matter what your personal approach to expectations and actions, never surrender your vision of students' true growth.

This assumes a fine but important line of distinction between expectations and vision. What we expect of students are those relatively tangible things that we can explain, put on paper, and reinforce through our daily words and actions. They can be checked and measured, evaluated, and reevaluated. We may decide to lower our expectations about a new project when we see that all students are struggling to the point of diminishing returns, or we may raise our expectations when we realize that students are accomplishing tasks without putting forth 100 percent effort. What we expect of students can shift frequently and dramatically depending on circumstances and results.

We may state specific expectations to students. We map out big ideas, smaller objectives, and daily activities to prompt their learning. We check their understanding and skills in objective, tangible, reportable ways. We maintain pacing and sequencing to move them along swiftly toward clearly defined goals. Students know our expectations well and either fulfill or fail to meet them. We declare students proficient and prepared to move on to the next level, or deem that they need to repeat the material.

Vision, on the other hand, refers to a long-term, holistic, and relatively abstract sense of how we hope students develop in our class and beyond. It is much more difficult, if not impossible, to define or assess. It is not constricted to particular subject matter, nor is it demonstrable through a predetermined set of skills or actions. We may stab at it with phrases like "becoming their best selves" or "being fully human," but words fail to capture it fully. Vision seems to be both universal and intensely personal at the same time. After all, they are *my* students in *my* class right now, right? And yet our vision for them involves an unfolding story so much bigger than our humble classroom in our little school in our particular community.

Students may meet, or not meet, our expectations and we might adjust them based on class dynamics. Expectations are initially firm, yet ever adaptable. They work splendidly for monitoring, testing, and disseminating students' particular advances according to pre-established curricular guidelines. They also can include classroom behaviors and social standards. They can be shared and discussed among colleagues. Deeper down, though, is a vision for students that cannot be adequately described or debated. It takes all you have, and you are the only one that can see it. See it clearly, and even if expectations get dashed to the ground, never surrender that vision.

KEY IDEAS:

- Consider how expectations may differ from vision in your own perspective.
- Explore your deepest sense of vision for students' overall growth. Only you can do so.

LEARNING IS EASY UNTIL STUDENTS ARE CONVINCED OTHERWISE

Learning is one of our specialties as human beings. We do it from day one and throughout life, sometimes of necessity, sometimes because we are required, and sometimes out of pure joy and personal interest. Learning comes rather naturally to us when it is relevant and helpful in our lives. We want to find out how to make things work easier and better for ourselves and our loved ones. We want to solve the problems that arise in our lives with knowledge of tools and relevant skills. We want to explore new materials and events that may have special meaning for us or bring us unique enjoyment. Our learning in these situations is relatively easy, a simple logical process that takes us from Point A to Point B. So, when and where do we pick up the idea that learning is difficult?

Usually, in school. At some point along the way, a teacher tells us that a concept, project, or skill is going to be really tough to grasp or complete. Other teachers chime in with similar sentiments, and older peers confirm the worst with their war stories from last year. The verdict is clear: Learning is now hard.

Is there really *ever* a good reason to tell someone that what they are about to learn will be difficult? Some teachers may want to give students fair warning, to prepare them for the worst, to give them an honest prediction. Others may proclaim difficulty because they may have faced, or even still face, challenges with the concept or skill themselves. Still others may do it simply because "some things need to be difficult for students in school. It's good for them." These reasons are all understandable but none of them seems to justify dismantling the beautiful, natural way of learning with which we all started.

Is it possible to offer students fair warning about the complexity of a concept more subtly, simply by publicizing the length of time the class will spend on it or the number of assignments associated with it? Is it possible to hone your own skills such that everything you teach is *well* within your skills set, making you more likely to project a more relaxed and confident attitude to students? Is it possible to reevaluate the need to push students dramatically through "difficult" learning circumstances to prepare them for real life, and perhaps help them weed the word out of their personal vocabulary instead? In other words, is it necessary to label certain educational experiences as especially difficult or could we allow learning to just be learning, all the time?

Babies, infants, and toddlers do not seem to label any of their learning experiences as difficult; we may observe them to be so, but that is our problem. This is not to suggest that we sugarcoat our communications to students, pretending that everything will be a breeze. Let us just let learning be learning and see what happens. It is really pretty easy, until students are convinced otherwise.

KEY IDEAS:

- Humans learn rather effortlessly early on and teachers can embrace that momentum.
- Speculation about learning can disrupt the learning itself; let it happen naturally.

WISE EDUCATORS REALIZE THAT STUDENTS
ARE THEIR OWN BEST TEACHERS

You are "the teacher," a separate, different human being, naturally observed to be at some physical distance by the students. You are expected to bring all sorts of external goods into their lives: materials, ideas, perspectives, examples, and activities. You are charged with passing along your expertise through carefully sequenced demonstrations and explanations; yet, beneath it all, your coordinated efforts really serve only to fuel minds that are teaching themselves. Looking at the classroom this way can have dramatic effects on the way you approach students. Do you see your students as their own best teachers?

The power of being one's own best teacher lies in the fact that complete teaching-learning cycles can take place within a single mind, yielding a highly integrated process and impressive results. A very practical example might help illustrate. Music students studying instruments like piano and drums face the challenge of trying to match their two hands for equal technique. Most people consider themselves to have a dominant hand and a non-dominant hand, and can readily prove it. As music students move through exercises to strengthen their non-dominant hand and bring it up to par, they can use a simple built-in strategy: modeling it on their dominant hand. Repeatedly checking what the dominant hand is doing correctly serves as the impetus for "teaching" the non-dominant hand how to do it. The strength of this approach is that the cycle *modeling-observation-trial-error-modeling-observation-trial-improvement* is all happening within that single student's body and mind. No external explanations, demonstrations, or feedback are necessary. The hand imbalance is gradually fixed "in house."

The same can apply to learning all sorts of concepts and skills. The questions to ask are, "What related concepts and skills have students already mastered, in my subject or others?" and "How can that mastery be used in self-teaching a given new concept or skill?" Hopefully, these questions are gradually transferred from teacher to students, so that they become, "What related concepts and skills have *I* already mastered, in this subject or others?" and "How can that mastery be used to teach *myself* this new concept or skill?" As students take on this mentality, they widen and deepen their own learning and become more independent along the way.

As an example, science students may be learning to wire basic circuitry. You, the teacher, know that the tangible outcome of today's lesson is that students should be able to assemble a number of smaller parts such that a small LED will illuminate. You have at least two choices, with lots of variations in between: (1) show them how to do it, step-by-step, or (2) review the basic concepts they have learned and send them off for self-teaching. In the first approach, the external source provides the information, lists the order of events, and probably models everything as students proceed. Everyone's product will likely work the same, but many students will probably need to be shown again if they are to replicate the project later.

In the second approach, students are forced to teach themselves how to make it work, drawing on what they have already mastered and applying it to what is needed to solve the problem. Students' products might differ in small details, but achieve the same stated goal. They will likely be able to complete the task again in the future the same way—or even in a different successful way—because they have used their own minds as a source of information, transfer, application, and creativity. They have not only discovered the real point of the project, which is crucial learning in and of itself, but also have increased the likelihood that they could successfully complete it again. Finally, they are also more likely to be able to craft a functional circuit in the future by themselves simply because they have already done it *by themselves*. A subtle but powerful voice says, "I have accomplished this on my own before; I can do it again."

So, what does the teacher do while students are self-teaching? Is your job finished for the day once you decide to turn over the circuit learning responsibility? Probably not. That is the point when the real decision-making begins. Students call you over to ask for clarification. Do you give them a brilliant and clear answer or put the ball right back in their court? Students are about to take a wrong turn, one that you can see will require them to start all over. Do you save the day or leave some extra space for real learning? There are no correct answers to these questions; your decisions depend on factors like safety, time, and students' dispositions.

Laying out the steps for an activity and walking students meticulously through each can be tempting, because it tends to yield convenient, convergent results. Nudging students toward self-teaching can be a messier process with divergent results. The first way may be more efficient, but the second way probably reflects real life more accurately. When professionals do their work successfully, rarely are they following a specific script prepared and presented by someone else. Instead, they use what they know to craft *appropriate* solutions: "How do I balance the company's budget to build in extra funding for a needed project?"; "How do I plumb this room to maintain easy access to the water line while avoiding electrical wires?"; or "How can I present this court case to ensure the fairest outcome for my client?" A handful of the best CFOs, plumbers, or lawyers would probably devise different solutions for these problems, but all with a successful outcome as stated. If problem-solving is to be learned in school, students have to *actually face problems*, and by solving them again and again, more and more independently, they come to realize that they are their own best teachers. What a gift.

KEY IDEAS:

- Self-teaching is powerful learning because the entire cycle happens internally.
- Convergent thinking is neat and clean, but divergent thinking can yield independence.

BE A GREAT STUDENT

As a teenager, I worked in the kitchen of a seafood restaurant. A major component of the training for any new employee there was to spend one entire shift shadowing each position: host, bartender, barback, waiter, back waiter, dishwasher, and line cook. It was a great way to introduce every team member to the whole operation and also instill some sympathy for each other's daily work. As a back waiter, one was much less likely to hastily sling a pile of dirty dishes all over the sink area if he knew what it felt like to be inundated as a dishwasher. As a waiter one would think twice before hollering for a late meal from the kitchen staff, knowing what it feels like to have a line of order tickets a mile long. I was a big fan of this training method; in fact, I always thought it would be helpful to require it again once in a while throughout an employee's tenure there.

As teachers, we have already experienced many years of this type of training in school, getting to know what it is like on the other side of the table as students. Not only have we amassed at least twelve to sixteen years of formal education, we have endured it in different buildings with a diverse array of teachers and fellow student cohorts. In fact, all high school graduates could be said to be experts on school and studenthood; teachers simply choose to turn that experience into a primary resource for their career work.

Drawing on your past experiences as a student to inform your work as a teacher is not automatic, though. You probably have found that you need to reflect purposefully, asking questions of yourself and exploring past experiences in detail, to gain full benefits from your "inherent" knowledge. You may run into a challenge as a teacher, knowing that somewhere in the dark recesses of your mind lies the solution, but need a few moments to really think it through and use what you discovered for yourself those many years ago.

As in the restaurant example, we could also benefit from repeated "student training" for teachers periodically throughout our careers. When practicing teachers assume the role of students again we develop a renewed compassion for what it is like to be in their shoes. We gain a much better perspective than we ever could have as an "original" student because now we have taught, giving us true vision from both sides. We get plenty of reminders and new insights about why students respond the way they do, what makes them tired or bored, how pacing functions from their viewpoint, and what it feels like to do group assignments again, for example.

Most teachers, especially in public schools, are required to complete additional coursework or degrees once they have begun formal teaching. The stated purpose of these mandates usually entails something like "learning additional research-based knowledge and skills appropriate to one's discipline." While this is important to help keep us current, another purpose might be something like "reacquainting themselves directly with all aspects of studenthood through older, wiser eyes." This second reason could be every bit as important as the first.

The benefits we gain from being a student again depend greatly on our attitude and approach. This may come as a shock to you, but every once in a great while a teacher will show up to an administrator-planned in-service presentation with a slightly less than enthusiastic attitude. Why? We're tired. We have a lot to do. We have been in these sessions before and not learned a whole lot. We think we already know it all. We know how these guest presenters are, and are already not impressed. We don't like moving into breakout groups to discuss what the presenter thinks is a great idea.

Sound familiar? Aren't these the sorts of feelings our students may be facing every single day? Now, what if you were to head in to every student experience just like you wish your own students would? The next time you take a night class, or attend an in-service, or go to a conference session, stride in like the student you would love to have in class. Show up with a fresh mind and spirit, ready to seize the day, work well with others, and exit the room a much-improved version of who entered.

Each of us has our own idea of what makes ideal students. If we all listed the traits we would love to see we would probably find lots of similarities but also lots of differences. Try actually listing those traits. What would a roomful of top-notch students look like for you? Get to the heart of that list and then *be one of those students*. Doing so will probably help you enjoy your student experiences more. It will also be a great gift to your instructor, and it might just rub off somehow on your students when you go back to work. Keep in touch with the student side of things; better yet, make the most of it.

KEY IDEAS:

- Returning to studenthood periodically is only as worthwhile as we make it.
- Decide for yourself what makes a great student and embody it all the time.

STUDENTS KNOW GENUINE—AND PHONY—WHEN THEY SEE IT

Most teachers probably readily agree that being genuine with our students is important. We should approach them in a natural way, reflecting our true and unique attitudes and dispositions throughout our interactions. We should say what we mean and mean what we say. Students should know our stance on important issues in the classroom, have a sense of our teaching philosophy and top priorities, and feel confident they can trust our leadership, one human being to another. If these things are in place, school runs relatively well for all involved; if something phony crops up, students sniff it out immediately.

The question to ask yourself is probably not whether you are mostly a phony most of the time, but rather whether you might have an occasional "phony moment" here and there, perhaps without even realizing it. We entertain a number of influences and perceived pressures on a regular basis in our jobs. To make things work well, we must be willing to reach healthy compromises with colleagues, administrators, parents, and students regularly. Coming to agreements and being an effective team player in your school means being flexible and open-minded, but it should not corner you into doing something that feels fake or false, especially in the classroom.

For instance, say you are required to administer a new standardized test during class next month. You will miss valuable minutes with your students to walk them through a seemingly irrelevant assessment, the value of which you are not yourself convinced. In fact, nobody in the school—students, colleagues, and maybe even administrators—seems to be especially enthused about it. Your administrators have asked you to set up the test in a positive light, encouraging your students to have a good attitude going in. You feel the phony coming on.

You have at least three choices in a situation like this: carry on cheerily in a way that feels fake to you, express your true opinions publicly regardless of students' resultant attitudes, or use the entire situation as an opportunity for everyone to grow. The first option is probably the worst. Students have a keen eye for phony, and though deep down they probably prefer to follow you respectfully as a genuine teacher, they are more than willing to call you out as one who is not. Being phony about something often borders on outright lying, territory that we certainly never want to cross with our students.

The second option may be a bit better, but still not very helpful. If something is truly outrageous, dangerous, or otherwise contemptible, we need to make a public point in front of students and do everything we can to bring about change. If, on the other hand, it is something we feel is not quite right and just needs to be adjusted we should perhaps watch our words. In the case of the standardized exam, badmouthing it entirely might just be a waste of time and a distraction to students, not especially conducive to their learning.

The third option is to seek any potential good in the situation, highlight it, and use what we see as the negative parts to make some valuable points. Does the exam administration offer opportunities for students to learn more deeply about the education system that produced it, the way the assessment is created, revised, and scored, or the reasons the assessment has been adopted at your school? Can they discover through the experience additional insights about their personal educational paths long-term, or their own practical test-taking skills right now? We can state our opinions about the test in a reasonable, honest, and professional manner while also using the moment to generate learning—potentially valuable learning that might never have come about without it.

This is about more than just trying really hard to see the silver lining. That can quickly become phony too. It is about simply recognizing *what is* in school situations, choosing to see it as fully and broadly as possible, and handling it in genuine, mature ways. If you look deeply, you would probably find it to be false to say either "This test is going to be really great!" *or* "This test is totally worthless." Be honest, with yourself and with students, to see things as clearly as possible and make the most of the opportunity. In the example, being genuine as a teacher probably goes far above and beyond a simple "yes/no" or "agree/disagree" decision on your part.

Other bits of phony we should seek and destroy might be small, subtle moves we make that slip under the radar but leave a hint of uneasiness. Students' responses will be your best indicator. If they sense you are faking something even a bit they tend to pick up on it and reflect it back. Do you occasionally decide to be the strict disciplinarian, demanding absolute focus and conformance when that is really not your style? Or the opposite, trying to be Mr. or Ms. Cool, letting things slide when it is actually eating you up inside? Maybe you take on a certain voice inflection or facial expression habitually with a certain group of students that you never use otherwise? Perhaps you put on your "highly professional" air in response to a classroom challenge, knowing inside that you should be rolling up your sleeves and solving it instead.

Let that scary word "phony" ring in your ears when it should, to help you weed out every little bit of it. Pay attention to students' behaviors that might be subtly reflecting that you compromised your own genuine nature for a moment. Our students know genuine, and phony, when they see it; we should too.

KEY IDEAS:

- Being consistently genuine in our interactions with students builds healthy relationships.
- Eliminating phony moments can be difficult but rewarding work; be open and honest.

DISCOVER WHAT YOUR STUDENTS *ACTUALLY NEED*

We seem to use the phrase "student needs" rather frequently, and sometimes carelessly, in education. Naturally, teachers want to discover what they can offer their students and devise creative ways to deliver it. Sometimes, though, we may be confusing *need* with *want*. If we do, we run the risk of providing for their wants but perhaps not actually meeting their needs: slight distinction, big mistake.

Several sources of information can inadvertently mislead us when determining what students actually need. The first is students themselves. They may think they know the end goal, and what is necessary to get there, but they have not actually developed the big-picture perspective to see clearly enough yet. As experts in both subject matter and human development, a big part of our job is to monitor students' engagement of the material closely enough that we can see how much help to offer in a given moment. Students may think they need nothing, that they have it all figured out, that the topic is a "done deal." You may have the perspective in that moment to recognize that what they need is a little more perspective! On the other hand, students may feel that they need lots of help, so-called "hand holding," to get through an activity or challenge, when in fact what they really *need* is for you to say "On your own this time around. You can do this!"

A related misleading source of information is students that have gone before this year's class. If you are teaching the same concept or skill the same way you have taught it for the past few years, you probably have a preconceived notion of where students will need the most help and how you can give it to them to avoid troubles. However, you may find that this year's group is different in every way, including the actual needs they have to make the project a success. This is a challenging but rewarding balance to strike, using what you know from previous classes to inform your planning, while maintaining an open mind about the students sitting before you and the unique gaps they may present in learning.

A third source of potentially distracting information is what others say your students need. "Others" could be virtually anyone—colleagues, friends, experts in the field, parents, administrators, textbook authors, or past college professors. All of these constituents, even when they bring excellent perspectives and rationales, and truly have your students' best interests in mind, can be mistaken about the particular needs in your class. Again, we must consistently seek the best possible combination of what "really should work" and what is actually needed. Bear in mind that sometimes you can engage these helpers in an ongoing conversation. If their initial ideas do not seem to apply or function well in your class, be willing to go back to them and explain the situation; they may have further perspectives to offer based on their experience and unique vantage point.

Finally, the sneakiest of all—we can be misled about students' actual needs simply by what *we predicted* they would need. If you are teaching a new class or a new topic within an existing class, you make lots of predictions. How much baseline knowledge will students have? How fast should pacing proceed through specific units and overall? What should students truly gain from this course that might not be visibly apparent on the surface? And, what will their specific needs be of me?

Asking yourself these sorts of questions is crucial for a good start in the course, and they will require some educated guessing to arrive at useful answers. Some of them, including attention to students' needs, will also require continuous monitoring and adapting. This vigilance will be most effective if you are able to suspend your predictions in the moment, keep them at arm's length, and perceive clearly what students actually need from you as they proceed each step along the way.

We can also make false predictions on a short-term basis. As you finish today's lecture-demonstration on identifying adverbial phrases you may think that students will need lots of practice going through a series of steps to do it themselves. If the truth of the matter is that they could easily do ten of them right now, then what they actually need is for you to cut them loose and put them to work. On the contrary, we might think that students are completely ready for their adverbial phrase homework tonight when, in fact, what they actually need is a bit more practice as a group with your guidance. Other possibilities for what they actually need might be examples from a related grammatical concept, a short video to serve as a reference when they work at home, or a mnemonic to recall the steps you taught them. Be responsive and creative.

Let us close with an important note about students' "other" needs, that is, those vital personal and psychological considerations beyond class content. These needs can also take many forms and can also come with misleading indicators. Do students need to be pushed hard? Do they need constant praise? Do they need individual recognition in front of the class from time to time? *All* the time? Do they need healthy competition? Individual work time? Group collaboration and comradery? Do they need you to circulate and check in over their shoulder? To go away and let them struggle for success? To give them an example from your own life? To leave them alone? Pay close attention to your students' actual needs for those larger goals in your educational environment too. You may be the only one that can clearly see them.

KEY IDEAS:

- What students want and what they need can be two very different things.
- Predicting and planning for students' needs should be balanced with readiness to adapt.

OUR JOB IS TO CHALLENGE STUDENTS WITHOUT OVERWHELMING THEM, AGAIN AND AGAIN

That's it. Just figure out, time after time, how hard to push students to induce maximum growth without breaking them. Teachers have many ways to boil the excessive details of their work down into very simple statements of job description. This is one of them.

Of course, the many applications of this clear-cut little compass are what make teaching so complex. The trick is to keep your focus on this simple balance when things start to get messy. Distractions abound and problems arise. The question remains: Are you challenging students without overwhelming them?

If you aren't challenging students thoroughly, you can't possibly overwhelm them—a good, safe approach, but one that does not yield much progress. If you are overwhelming students you cannot be challenging them appropriately anymore; they have reached the point of no return. What, then, are factors that contribute to a well-calibrated challenge?

We need to exercise our powers of observation, vision, and creativity to make the most of challenges for students. Observation entails paying close attention to all the details of what already is. At this moment in real time. What, exactly, have students learned thus far? How are they participating in class activities right now? How are they doing on homework assignments and quizzes? What are they talking about as they enter and exit your room? What do their facial expressions and physical movements betray as you ask a question or introduce a new topic? How quickly, or slowly, are they handling new information? What additional, up-to-date observational information can you gather from parents, other teachers, aides, or tutors? The librarians? The main office staff? The bus drivers? Gathering as much pertinent data as possible will help you see clearly where students currently are.

Second, we need vision for what students could possibly turn out to be. That is, as a result of whatever challenges we end up putting in their path, how will they turn out in the end? Teachers must be fabulous imaginers. We have to keep one foot firmly planted in practical matters and rational thinking while the other explores the entire realm of possibilities for the people under our charge. How might your students turn out in your wildest educator fantasies? If everything were truly possible, and they could really be anything they wanted to be in every way? These questions can be answered in large, lofty terms or according to very specific learning outcomes. Spending some time and energy on the vision aspect of crafting appropriate challenges is well worth it.

Finally, we need creativity to make the most of our challenges to students. We cannot expect that something that has already been manufactured, produced, or published will provide the perfect challenge level for them. It is possible, occasionally, but unlikely. Rather, building on keen observation and vivid vision we must be prepared to generate original challenges, or substantial adaptations of existing ones, to nudge our novice fliers to the edge of the cliff without pushing them over. Beware the tendency to put forth only preconceived ideas and materials, expecting them to somehow hit the spot. Be ready to stop short, step on the gas, or take a sharp turn to make sure students continue to give all they have without wearing out. Finding that point, again and again, is a constant process. And an exciting job.

KEY IDEAS:

- Students learn best by being challenged appropriately.
- Crafting ideal challenges requires observation, vision, and creativity.

INTRINSIC MOTIVATION IS ALWAYS BETTER THAN THE ALTERNATIVE

Why? Because it comes from within the very people that are the focus of education. When students approach learning with motivation already welling up from the inside out, they are optimally primed for progress. It is akin to having food in the belly rather than out in the fields, or air in the lungs rather than up in the atmosphere, or as the old saying goes, one bird in the hand rather than two in the bush. While this famous statement usually points to a slightly different meaning, it describes the relationship between intrinsic and extrinsic motivation beautifully. The former is always preferable to the latter.

We have all seen intrinsic motivation at work in students: the eighth grader who writes a polished piece of software in the computer lab during flex period, the kindergartener who makes an additional art project better than the one we assigned, or the track athlete who shows up early to school to run a few laps before homeroom. Not required, unexpected, above and beyond, golden. These are people putting themselves in situations that are not prescribed and will not be rewarded. They often will not be noticed at all; in fact, many students in these situations purposefully keep their actions quiet. They just do their work, steadily and passionately, reaping the internal satisfaction it brings.

Furthermore, students often do not even recognize their own satisfaction after accomplishing something internally motivated. It just happens. Outsiders may ask them about their feelings or reactions to a self-initiated project, or what drove them to do it in the first place, to which they shrug their shoulders honestly and humbly and say, "I don't know, I just did it." They have not knowingly accepted even internal rewards, much less external ones. They contributed something to their world just because it arose within them.

The opposite, extrinsic motivation, is a big part of education. The rewards are plainly evident in systems like points for assignments, grades on report cards, and posted exam scores in numerical order. Teachers use competitions and showcases to encourage students to put forth their best work and to mutually maintain high standards and expectations among themselves. Extrinsic rewards may be subtler, too: a quick smile from the teacher for correct answers, unpublicized placement in line according to behavior in class, or calling on the raised hands of high achievers. Whether intentional or not, these moves nudge students in a certain direction from the outside. Students learn to behave and perform in specific ways in each classroom based on their expectation of a payoff of some kind. People are learning to accomplish tasks for rewards.

One might argue that this is the way "real life" works. We accomplish tasks for rewards. True. However, we also accomplish tasks purely from intrinsic motivation, and the results can be surprising and wonderful. A few real-world examples witnessed recently are:

- The set designers at the professional theater who bemoan the hard work required for the upcoming production, but spend countless voluntary hours on a self-initiated backdrop for a themed cast party.
- The housing contractor who polishes off a long day's construction work by building a training prop for free at the local firehouse.
- The police officer who spontaneously composes a full-fledged musical that eventually makes it to Broadway.

These people took up the torch of their own volition, accomplishing and producing wonderful things unexpectedly—neither necessarily planning to do so nor expecting anything in return.

So, how do we handle intrinsic and extrinsic motivation with our students? Attempting to actually prompt or encourage intrinsic motivation would be oxymoronic and probably impossible, but simply making room for it can be helpful. Noticing it as it begins to manifest in students and quietly providing the time and space for it to take hold may be highly helpful to its fruition. For example, are you the one that determines whether and how students can use that computer lab during flex period? Do you determine whether those kindergarteners are allowed to use more art materials than the original allotment? Do you have the key to the locked fence around that running track? And what time do you tend to arrive in the morning? Paying attention to these little things and silently facilitating the intrinsic motivation you see developing in students can make all the difference.

You might also create space for students' intrinsic motivation by eliminating some extrinsic motivations under your purview. Do students need to get points for every little thing they do? Does "extra credit"-type work have to involve credit? Do you have to respond to every contribution with a positive acknowledgment? Do all outstanding grades have to be published? Do self-initiated efforts have to be recognized in front of the group? These are questions to ask yourself on a case-by-case basis, of course. Doing so may help you invite intrinsic motivation into balance with its alternative more frequently and effectively.

KEY IDEAS:

- Intrinsic motivation is self-sustaining but can be supported in subtle ways.
- Watching for intrinsic motivation can help us balance it with the alternative regularly.

SKILLS ARE MORE IMPORTANT THAN CONTENT

We plan lots of content for students—facts, terms, dates, names, detailed concepts, and big ideas. No matter the students' level of advancement in our curriculum, there is always plenty more "stuff" to learn. In fact, the further they go the more the heap of new content seems to grow. Teachers maintain a dual sense of students' current position and how much material is left to learn; sometimes, it feels like the gap is enormous. Where do we even start?

The danger of thinking too much about content is that we may come to objectify it. That is, we may start to think of all those facts and ideas as a *thing* that we are forking over to students in as wise a way as possible. To keep your attention focused on the people in front of you, try placing prime priority on skills rather than content. What are the skills people should master to be successful in environmental science, sports medicine, journalism, or dance and how are we helping them build those skills in our courses, be they highly specific Advanced Placement classes in high school or related fundamental classes in elementary school?

The advantage of focusing on skills is that they require the direct engagement of human beings on a relatively holistic level. When students learn only content they perceive, assimilate, and remember, but do not necessarily apply and practice, and especially not with a combination of visual, aural, and kinesthetic faculties. The line of distinction is not perfectly clear, but usually absorbing content and exercising skills are two very different processes; a focus on skills tends to produce more thorough, lasting, and practically useful results.

One might argue that some mastery of content is necessary to develop related skills. Therefore, aren't they equally important? Though skills are dependent on requisite knowledge, the relationship between the two actually further reinforces the logic of placing highest priority on skills. The knowledge serves the skills, and not vice versa. This is, in fact, a great gauge when learning both; if skills have been learned well one should easily be able to observe inherent content mastery also. On the other hand, if we teach only for content mastery, we cannot assume that students have also learned the related skills.

In math, for example, learning what decimals are and how they affect numbers is helpful only insofar as students can *use* them skillfully to calculate and monitor baseball batting averages or banking interest rates. Correct execution of the skills automatically implies understanding of decimals per se, but the opposite is not necessarily true. Answering some questions about decimals or solving a few test problems does not necessarily imply understanding of how to apply decimals in relevant ways. Similarly, learning all of the parts of speech and even identifying them in real sentences is worthwhile, but only if students can actually apply that knowledge toward better reading and writing. Can they use the content they have mastered to put the pieces of their own communication in a logical, clear flow that captures readers' attention? As another example, remembering key principles of staging, lighting, and costuming is important for understanding theatrical production, but can students actually put these principles to work in producing a small piece themselves?

A great way to describe the contrast between content and skills is "not learning *about* science, but learning science" or "not learning *about* sculpture, but learning sculpture." What does it mean to really "learn science"? It means using factual information to explore the processes that help us understand our world better—in other words, to master skills that demonstrate knowledge acquisition but also bring it to life through our personal efforts. Surely all teachers require students to learn and demonstrate skills rather than just knowledge sometimes, but perhaps we could seek opportunities to favor the former over the latter more often. Consider how frequently your students are truly "learning" your subject, rather than "learning about" it.

KEY IDEAS:

- Skill mastery usually assumes knowledge mastery, but not necessarily vice versa.
- Helping students conquer the skills in our field can help them see its purpose from within.

THINGS ARE USUALLY EASIER THE SECOND
TIME AROUND

This old phrase has been used in numerous applications. The inherent wisdom is rather obvious; once we have already done something we have a better idea of how it works, what is required, what can go wrong, and how we can accomplish the task more successfully next time. The phrase also implies that the first time we do anything is usually the toughest. We harbor some fear of the unknown; we have to estimate important things like projected time and energy consumption; and we are concerned about whether the plan will actually work. The first time around entails risk; the second usually involves confidence honestly earned.

Teachers face many challenging first times in our careers. The very first time we stand in front of our own class as the sole "adult in the room." The first time we give a test and grade it. The first time we have to call a parent meeting. The first time we get stuck in a learning sequence. The first time we encounter a logistical or pedagogical conflict with a colleague or administrator. The first time we introduce a rather adventurous activity in class. The first time we put students in charge of their own small groups. The first time we lead a large-scale field trip. Most of these will happen more than once in your career, and all are usually easier to handle the second time around.

This segment is not just a feel-good "It's going to be okay" pep talk, though it may serve that purpose in some cases. The point is not only to focus on how much better the second time will be, if we can just survive to that point. Rather, the goal is to be proactive about *how you engage those first times*. Are there ways to set up a given initial experience in your career so that it is less daunting and more fruitful? Can you time an event such that you will be best prepared to see it through successfully? Can you approach a potentially difficult meeting with a clear head and noble intentions? Can you analyze possible outcomes of an interaction to be ready to take the next step once the "main event" has transpired? Can you plan a complicated activity or assessment such that students, and you, will gain big benefits from the experience no matter what? Tackling questions like these beforehand can help you approach the onset with better ideas and a healthier attitude.

Often, what complicates our first times is that they come as a surprise. A great way to prepare yourself for these situations is to pay attention to your colleagues. Notice what they are doing, listen to their stories, ask them questions, and find out what you can about their first times in various school experiences. What may seem like annoying complaints in the faculty lunchroom, for instance, can turn into valuable information that helps you avoid similar pitfalls in the future. Be open to suggestions and eager to listen. In some cases, their first time around can prepare you most of the way toward making your first feel like your second.

If things are usually easier the second time around, it would seem to follow that they become even easier the third time, fourth time, and so on. When it comes to parent meetings or administrator challenges, for example, this is usually the case. However, be careful when planning classroom activities. The fourth and fifth time, for example, may contribute to a stale environment. In other words, you can reach a point where you have done something so many times with so many classes of students that it becomes a little too easy and too familiar. These feelings can lead to boredom, which students detect immediately. Honor each student's right to an inspiring education by consistently tackling new firsts on a regular basis. The very risks you take can prompt a fresh excitement in the room, seemingly inexplicable and perhaps recognized only by you, but enjoyable to everyone.

Speaking of students, the easier-the-second-time effect applies to them too. We probably all have heard students doubt their own abilities, worry about the outcome of their projects, or hesitate to offer a new and untested idea. We probably all have seen them struggle with something we know is easily within their reach and that will be automatic for them a week, month, or year down the road. We can remind them that it is good to face challenges and learn from mistakes, but our words may be empty if we are not tackling lots of firsts with a positive attitude ourselves.

Examine your approach to firsts, tackle them like you hope your students would, and share those experiences openly with them. Take inspiration from watching your students face firsts themselves and then be sure to enjoy the second time around together. What a shame it would be to survive the first time and then move right along without reinforcing the accomplishment via a second, easier, better pass. Doing so helps students experience the relationship between trial, error, correction, improvement, and success. Along the way, they pick up skills of courage, persistence, awareness, self-reflection, analysis, and wise judgment. Not a bad lesson.

KEY IDEAS:

- First experiences may be scary and challenging but we can prepare ourselves for them.
- Help students learn to embrace firsts, perhaps directly through your modeling.

THERE'S NO SUCH THING AS SCIENCE OR HISTORY, JUST *PEOPLE* DOING SCIENTIFIC AND HISTORICAL THINGS

As the age-old saying goes, "We don't teach math [or dance or language arts], we teach people." In other words, math and dance and language arts do not exist by themselves as objective things; they take on meaning only through the actions of students. The devil's advocate will ponder a number of items that could represent an objective, stand-alone subject matter: a famous text-book, an official curriculum document, or an online grade book full of assignments, assessments, and scores. None of these means anything by itself. They all point toward *students* doing, for example, scientific and historical things.

This perspective is a reflection of "real life" as well. Law and medicine and sports psychology do not exist as "fields" in and of themselves. They are convenient ways of categorizing the sort of work that people have chosen to do. All too often, we seem to forget this, referring to various professions and areas of study as if they were "things" out there that people can choose to engage. The truth is that each field is constantly evolving according to the actions of the professionals that embody, sustain, and improve it.

This has profound implications for the way we approach our students through the knowledge and skills of our subject matter. We are not teacher-people trying to help student-people grasp some object out there called World History, German, or Earth Science. We are instead trying to mold their humanness more broadly and deeply from the inside out by helping them see what it is like to act like a historian, communicate like a Berliner, or think like an environmental scientist.

Each of us is bound to have some students continue on to study our subject in more depth or even pursue a career in our field. For them, gathering the specific understandings and skills of our discipline is crucial. Perhaps even more important, though, is finding ways to shed light on these same understandings and skills to the majority that ultimately will not choose our field. What, exactly, are you offering to those many students who will never touch chemistry, Spanish, or economics again, except by occasional chance? Are you helping them expand and improve their overall thinking-and-doing skills through the activities you present in your classes? Are you approaching them as people doing chemical, linguistic, and financial things, rather than people attempting to crack the code of some boxed up subject matter an arm's length away? Are you regularly emphasizing the unique ways of thinking employed by experts in your particular area of study? Are you modeling that thinking fully and consistently for students' overarching benefit as developing humans?

It is perhaps more convenient to think of second-grade language arts or tenth-grade U.S. history as a self-contained box of stuff that we gradually open up for a new group of students each year. We spend valuable time customizing this "stuff" to make it that much more effective and engaging. We prepare it carefully, putting it in logical order so that as students open it they enjoy maximum benefits. Yet we cannot allow the box of stuff to become the focus. After all, there is no such thing as science or history, just *people* doing scientific and historical things. And people must show them how.

KEY IDEAS:

- Thinking of our subject matter as an objective "thing" is convenient but not inspiring.
- Part of our job is to help students *experience* how professionals in our field function.

STUDENTS DO WHAT THEY KNOW

Or stated more comprehensively, people do what they know. Students just happen to be a great example of people exhibiting extensive personal change for long periods of time under relatively close observation. Students learn new information, new skills, and new ways of being and then apply them to their lives in school and out. What students "know" comes to them in so many ways—through conversation, imitation, observation, extrapolation, and imagination, to name a few. What they do depends on what they have experienced in these and other ways, so paying attention to what they are coming to know under your supervision is a high priority.

A famous phrase you may have seen, often attributed to Boonaa Mohammed, says, "Don't wait for people to be kind. Show them how." This phrase speaks for itself and provides a great example of how we can influence what students come to know. More powerful still is the fact that we could substitute any number of words for "kind" to produce broad and impressive results. "Don't wait for people to be courageous. Show them how." "Don't wait for people to be proactive . . . to be organized, . . . creative, . . . imaginative, . . . conscientious, helpful, quick, passionate, strong, persistent, patient, or perceptive." If students do not brush up against these traits, we can hardly fault them for not exhibiting them. They just do what they know.

As the quote suggests, our modeling on a regular basis is a powerful way to introduce students to the traits and dispositions we wish for them, but other angles are available too. One of the most accessible is peer interactions. Students tend to get quickly and fully engaged in their peers' actions, for better or for worse, because their classmates are so parallel to them in so many ways. An adult teacher demonstrating strength or patience is one thing; a classmate doing so is quite another. Constantly observing and identifying the shiny spots in each of your students can help you capitalize on the example they can offer to their peers. Viewer discretion is advised as to how you orchestrate this. Sometimes, you can comfortably make a public example of a student in front of the class for everyone's benefit. At other times, you might pair or group students for activities subtly so that one's "good stuff" rubs off gradually on another, and perhaps vice versa.

A third way to facilitate what students come to know is by setting and maintaining the educational environment. Even if none of your students currently seems to "know" patience or open-mindedness or attention to detail, you can set up situations in which they will have to find those things within themselves by solving strategically placed problems. Guiding the development of these sorts of skills might be your real job description at any given point in time.

Finally, it is worth mentioning that students mostly *won't* do what they *don't* know. Imagine a child who has *never* heard a belittling comment, neither toward himself nor others. How would he know how to produce one himself? A child who has *never* experienced the idea "I can't" in any way? How could she possibly utter that herself? These, of course, are hypothetical examples unfortunately. But imagine it. What they have not yet come to know, they won't do.

Of course, students are learning throughout the day, not just in school, and certainly not just in your class, so they will come to know and do counterproductive things despite your best efforts. You cannot control their personal encounters with "I can't," for example, but you *can* influence their knowledge and exercise of "I can't" and "I can" in your room. By setting a consistent example yourself, grouping students wisely, and influencing the educational environment strategically, you can highlight what you hope students will come to experience and enjoy watching them do what they know.

KEY IDEAS:

- Students tend to generate what they have learned from experience.
- Teachers can influence students' school experiences for uniquely beneficial growth.

ENCOURAGE STUDENTS TO ASK "WHY?" FREQUENTLY

The five W's—who? what? when? where? why? Some teachers flip the third and fourth questions in their classroom activities, and some add "How?" as the "one H" or the "sixth W" (go figure!). In all cases, "Why?" seems always to come at the end of the string of the five W's. Perhaps it is the most advanced, and even important, of the questions.

The five W's are most often encountered as a framework for journalism, be it serious publishing projects or novice storytelling practice. The idea is to capture the details of a story fully, providing listeners or readers with a comprehensive set of facts to help them understand the situation. Students are encouraged to answer all five (or six) questions in their work.

These question words arise in school much more frequently than just in journalism practice, though. For example, teachers ask things like:

- Who played key roles in the civil rights movement of the mid-twentieth century?
- What are the primary, secondary, and tertiary colors?
- When is Earth closest to the sun every year?
- Where are the major arteries in the human body?

The answers to these questions are relatively objective. People may debate some of them slightly, but generally accepted responses can be posed, reinforced, remembered, tested, and reproduced rather simply. The last W remains.

Answering "Why?" takes time and effort. It is a messy affair, with ample opportunities for confusion, disagreement, and serious debate, all characteristics of a learning environment that is slightly scary and wonderfully fruitful. Ponder these examples of "Why?" questions related to each of the originals above:

- Why did each of these key figures choose to take up the fight?
- Why do these color categories matter in oil painting?
- Why is it coldest where I (or someone I know) lives at that point in time?
- Why are these arteries so crucial in first aid?

Each of these questions can push students way beyond their initial answers. They must incorporate other facts they may have learned, consider others' perspectives, and extrapolate responses based on all available information.

This may seem like a fairly simple process, and you may have discovered that you can answer each of these "Why?" questions with a relatively concise, widely acceptable answer. However, the beauty of asking "Why?" is that it gives us a chance to focus more on the asking than on the answering. It opens doors for extended thinking and additional exploration that the other W's generally cannot offer.

Consider, for example, the many avenues of discovery waiting behind the question "Why did each of these key figures choose to take up the fight?" Discussion might lead us to explore what our students consider to be worth fighting for today, why they have or have not done anything regarding the issue, whether civil rights is "finished business" in our nation, state, or local community, and why or why not. You may have noticed that "Why?" questions seem to yield additional "Why?" questions readily, a natural thinking process that produces accelerated student growth. Students can learn not only to answer your "Why?" questions thoughtfully and thoroughly, but to *ask their own.*

These are treacherous waters, of course. If our students start asking "Why?" frequently, what will become of classroom management? How will we stay on track? What if they ask a question we cannot answer? Or, worst of all, what if they even start to question *why* we are doing what we do in class? If students are asking their own "Why?" questions in a reasonably respectful way, you are definitely doing something right. None of these concerns should bother you enough to stop them. Be creative about when, where, and how students ask them. Aloud in front of the whole group? Taking turns individually in small groups? Individually in writing submitted to the teacher? And later shared anonymously with the class? Spontaneously when appropriate? Guided and expected on a given day?

In other words, *how* they ask their questions will determine, to a great extent, how well your classroom continues to function effectively in the midst of "Why?" exploration. Can you find ways to provide a vast amount of conceptual space for students to pose meaningful questions while also keeping the train on at least one track at all times? How far are you willing to let students stretch their cognitive muscles in order to engage the subject material in a truly inspiring way? Are you modeling your own "Why?" questions to the class on a regular basis? Do you ask an occasional question to which you have no idea what the answer may actually be? Do you honor their "Why?" questions by granting a bit of unexpected discussion time or shifting a pre-planned activity? Students determine very quickly how much priority teachers place on each of the five (or six) W's in class; they decide based on the actions we take on a regular basis. Encourage your students to ask "Why?" frequently. Show them how.

KEY IDEAS:

- "Why?" is a powerful tool for students' extended growth.
- Teachers may have to take some risks to create a healthy "Why?" environment.

~~DON'T~~ REINVENT THE WHEEL

The old saying, in its original form, reminds us that we should not put forth effort trying to devise or create something that has already been done. Why waste time struggling with questions and problems that someone else has already solved? Instead, we should pursue the next step, coming up with something new to benefit the world around us. Good advice, in general, but not always appropriate in education. Sometimes, our students should reinvent the wheel, and for great reasons.

The decision boils down to the contrast between breadth of learning and depth of learning. If our students take certain things for granted, immediately and on good faith, we can move on to other concepts efficiently, thus broadening their learning. We start with the wheel already invented, enabling us to explore ways to use it, modify it, or improve it. On the other hand, if we pursue an engaging way to require students to reinvent, or backwards-engineer, the assumed material we may be helping them to *deepen* their learning. That is, by making a wheel themselves they may be primed for learning or reinforcing physical concepts like friction, mass, and velocity. They may be readier to explore the history of machine technology and to fully grasp or apply another famous phrase: "Necessity is the mother of invention." They might explore how an odometer depends on a wheel, yielding additional opportunities to review geometrical concepts of circumference and diameter.

The metaphor has been carried sufficiently far here, but just notice that it actually presents us with a practical example. It may seem silly to make students reinvent a wheel, for example, or calculate a standard deviation, or rewrite code for something that comes standard in the latest gadget at the press of a button. However, in all of these cases the act of recreating what has already been done may offer students better insights not only into the content or product on display but also into ways of thinking that allowed humans to produce them in the first place. In other words, our students do not sit before us simply to be told what to do and then to produce it correctly, but to understand and *experience* how human beings conceive of and bring to fruition the amazing things they do. The beauty of this perspective on teaching and learning is that students not only master specific subject matter but also develop far-reaching healthy attitudes toward life-long learning and productive careers.

The obvious ensuing question is, "How many, and which, things do we reinvent?" Clearly, we could carry this approach too far and require students to start every concept and skill from scratch, wasting valuable time and effort. Sometimes assumptions need to be made and steps need to be skipped or only briefly mentioned, so that full, appropriate learning can flourish. However, an occasional reinvention can pave the way for very deep learning, as students experientially sympathize with the human thoughts and actions that have produced the progress we enjoy today. In fact, sometimes that full, appropriate learning depends completely on such an approach.

KEY IDEAS:

- Reinventing the wheel can be a great approach to paving the way for deeper learning.
- Balancing efficiency and experiential learning is an important teaching skill.

WHEN A STUDENT HAS A BETTER IDEA THAN YOUR OWN, SIT BACK AND ENJOY

After all, this is what school is for, right? Our wish is for students to have better and better ideas as they pass through our room and on to the next. We teachers like to think we are pretty smart. We have been through lots of school ourselves, studied our subject matter in depth, and contemplated the ins and outs of helping others learn it. And still, if we are doing things right, students will have better ideas than our own sometimes. Sit back and enjoy them.

What, exactly, does "sit back and enjoy them" mean? Many interpretations are possible, so here are a few examples to spark your imagination according to your style. You might step out of the conversation for a bit and let the student explain the idea more thoroughly to the class. You might pause for a few seconds with a genuine, wide grin and explain your reaction afterwards to celebrate the student's contribution publicly. You might carry on rather seamlessly with a quick acknowledgment in class but reflect on the moment later that evening, simply garnering some hope and inspiration from that student's recent growth. Any of these and many more are possibilities for a natural response to a beautiful moment.

Students are more likely to have, and share, their great ideas if we set up an atmosphere that is open and conducive, but more specifically, one that sends the message that students can have better ideas than teachers. We need to strike a healthy balance between both, of course, to maintain reasonable classroom order and pacing, so relishing occasional shining ideas can be just the right approach. In other words, students should not always have better ideas than ours—that would likely indicate a teacher problem—but they probably should have them at least once in a while, and we should make room to cherish those moments.

Teachers can help students learn to generate great ideas through a bit of proactive prompting too.

I recently had the opportunity to settle a mild dispute in our home. An expensive sports water bottle had been broken amid the shenanigans of our twin sons. Somehow I have been designated the judge in our house, expected by both wife and children to mete out fair and wise decisions about a rather wide variety of troubles. After hearing presentation of the evidence from all sides, including older-brother-witness, I told them I was happy to ponder a solution but first I would turn the tables. We would wait to hear a feasible, fair solution from each of our three sons before I proposed mine.

I like to think I had a good solution all along, but am quite pleased to report that they came up with a better idea by combining their individual suggestions.

Throughout the process, I gently bit my lip many times to keep from smiling wide, realizing that their final decision was going to be better than mine and that they were developing outstanding higher-order thinking skills in the process. They actually never asked again what my solution was until after the fact. They were focused on solving the problem rather than waiting for the sentence.

Teachers love to say that we hope our students will surpass us in various ways in our field. Are we setting the stage for that to happen? Do we offer an environment in which it is *likely* to happen? Do we acknowledge and celebrate ideas better than our own when they arise? A classroom atmosphere in which great ideas are welcomed and enjoyed is a wonderful place to be. For everyone.

KEY IDEAS:

- Consider if students' having better ideas than yours could be a top priority for your room.
- If so, allow natural, beautiful, enjoyable reactions to surface in those moments.

IN THE MIND, EVEN THE SKY IS NOT A LIMIT

Limits. Hmmm.

We certainly need them, as they help us stay in balance and function appropriately in the world around us. They define the forums in which we interact with others and help us act fairly and reasonably within those contexts. Limits can also bring trouble, though. They may box us in, restrict our natural tendencies, and curb our creativity. Exploring the nature of limits in our lives can help us engage them in helpful, purposeful ways and guide our students to do the same.

Limits arise externally and internally. Many external ones are non-negotiable, such as the time limits on your sixth-period class, the physical space allotted for you and your students to work every day, or the scope and sequence of material you can or should cover in a given course. You can defy any or all of these limits, but doing so might create a lot of trouble for your school community—not a great idea.

Other external limits are somewhat flexible and may invite you to question them. For example, limits on how you arrange your room, how you handle student hall passes, or how you incorporate technology in your teaching may all be subject to review and reevaluation. Discovering the need to update negotiable limits and taking action to create change in your school is an important part of faculty responsibility. Doing so in a professional manner also shows students how they might enact positive change in their lives at school and beyond.

Subtler still, and perhaps more powerful, than external limits are the internal ones we place on ourselves. Sometimes, without even realizing it, we tell ourselves that an idea we have is impossible, impractical, or just downright wacky. We may subconsciously limit our thoughts and plans according to our perception of the current culture of our school, the overarching guidelines and expectations of our curriculum, or the efficiency and progress typically expected and attained by others in our field. We may place these imaginary limits on ourselves or, worse yet, on our students:

> "I cannot take the class time to make that happen."
> "I just do not have that much energy."
> "The administration would never allow this to fly."
> "My students aren't ready for that yet."
> "My students don't think that way."
> "My students will never buy into this approach."

Where do all these limits actually reside? In our thoughts, of course. "Class time" and "student readiness" and "buy-in" are all concepts we entertain in our minds, and that is exactly where we must engage our internal limits if we want to challenge them. Think about how you think about allotted class time, for instance. Do you automatically place boundaries on it, assuming without question that a certain number of minutes on either end of a class period is useless because of students' entrance and exit? Do you implicitly accept the notion that class time is never sufficient? Consider how you gauge "student readiness." Does it derive to some extent from the performance of last year's students in the same course? Is it hedged by what you have heard from other teachers? Take a good look at student "buy-in." Do you predetermine what kindergarteners or sixth graders or high school seniors will be willing to try? Do you limit in your mind, before the moment of truth, the attitudes they might take toward a new frontier in your class?

The good news is that these highly powerful internal limits can be questioned, tested, and adjusted right within the same place they reside. Pushing against a perceived limit, or breaking it altogether, may later require external action to set things into motion, but the hardest work happens in the initial mental engagement itself. Once you push through that boundary in your mind, the rest tends to work itself out relatively easily.

The famous phrase reminds us that "the sky is the limit," that all of these things we may think are holding us or our students back are really not limits, that things are really much more open and infinitely possible than perhaps we imagine them to be. All of our internally imposed limits are just thoughts popping up in our minds; in fact, even our thoughts about those limits are just thoughts. We owe it to our students to question, investigate, and test those boundaries tenaciously. Students will benefit quite a bit from the external actions that our internal improvements produce and even more so from the example that sets for them. In the mind, even the sky is not a limit. Unless you say so.

KEY IDEAS:

- Recognizing limits and their levels of flexibility can help us engage them effectively.
- Internal limits can be harder to recognize and change, but don't let that stop you!

ABSENCE MAKES THE HEART GROW FONDER—
WITH STUDENTS, TOO

Maybe. This perspective is probably one of the most susceptible to debate in the whole book. We all have varying levels of desire to be around people, both when we compare ourselves to others and even within ourselves on a given day. Sometimes, we want to be surrounded by human life with all of its interesting, challenging, and entertaining characteristics. At other times, we need to be alone, even if only for a moment, to catch our breath, think things through, or release some tension. Absence is said to make hearts grow fonder in love relationships, but it can operate that way in school too.

Most teachers spend quite a bit of time with students every week, some even more than with their families, depending on school schedules and job descriptions. Besides standard class contact time, you may be meeting with students about grades or assignments, engaging them while on lunch duty, coaching a team or leading a club, or sponsoring or attending social events at school. You might see students around town, too, or attend non-school events to which they have invited you. All of these can be wonderful moments, but they can also add up to a feeling of personal contact overload for teachers. And students.

Pay attention to the times when you are extra enthusiastic about seeing your students. Is it after a long holiday weekend, or winter break? Does it shift or cycle depending on the time of year, the day of the week, or the combination of school activities in which you are involved? Are there times when you are glad to have a break or change, or when you wish you did? Or, are you highly enthusiastic about seeing all students all the time, no matter what?

Even if the latter is the case for you, still consider whether a bit of absence may be beneficial from time to time for two reasons. First, it might be healthy for you. You may feel excited about seeing your students again and again, and being thoroughly involved in every aspect of their lives, but that can wear you down over time and leave you less effective than you otherwise could be. Second, your students might need a bit of absence from you. They need some space sometimes and all too often they are not in control of seeking and finding it. Their days may be packed so tight, mostly by others, that they have no chance to withdraw for a moment to refresh, reevaluate, or realign. One little decision by you to give a student or students some room on a given day might make a big difference in their growth.

The indicators are all over, arriving both internally and externally. Simply put, whenever you feel a bit squeezed or overwhelmed by student interactions, find little opportunities to slow down, pull back, and catch your breath. Perhaps you choose to really just *monitor* the lunchroom one day instead of sitting and talking with lots of students as usual. Maybe you move swiftly down the hall one afternoon giving only warm, genuine smiles and waves rather than engaging numerous students in discussion or debate or playful banter. Perhaps you take a good look at your schedule to spread out the timing of extracurricular activities in which you are involved, to avoid having everything happen at once during the year. Maybe you shift gears on a given day to have all students do a bit of silent reading during class instead of launching into another teacher-driven activity. Any of these simple actions, and many more, can provide just the moment of peace you need to get yourself back on track and renew your enthusiasm for student interaction.

Similarly, watch for external indications that students may need a bit of absence from you. They might provide you with rather short responses or no response at all. They might show some frustration or appear overwhelmed by activities, assignments, or expectations for which you are the main source. If you see certain students very frequently in the course of a day or week, be especially attentive to indicators from them. If they seem like they need some space, by all means give it to them if feasible. You can always broach a topic again later, tomorrow or next week, or even after just a few minutes of retiring to your respective corners.

It is also certainly possible to be too absent. The heart will probably not grow fonder if there is little or no desire to be with students in the first place. Hopefully, we are not only highly enthusiastic about our interactions with them overall but also aware of the potential benefits of a bit of separation when the time is right. The frequency and duration of contacts with our students varies. We may see some of them relatively seldom, creating very little need to find extra space. Even then, in a given moment on a given day, a bit of absence might be exactly what works. The key is discovering, within constantly evolving relationships, *when* a bit of absence may make the heart grow fonder. Put this old phrase to the test once in a while to discover what works best for you. And them.

KEY IDEAS:

- Teachers have lots of contact time with students, sometimes more than we realize.
- Our enthusiasm can cause us to engage with them constantly, but can also overwhelm us.

Chapter 3

Your Moves

YOU CAN'T GIVE WHAT YOU DON'T HAVE

Teaching is a giving profession. We offer our students whatever we have, hoping that the experiences, perspectives, and problem-solving skills we possess in our field will be helpful to them as they learn the ropes. Even in our first years of teaching, we should have a wealth of experience from formal training and self-initiated study to give to our students in creative ways. Still, there are bound to be a few gaps in your repertoire, and you can't give what you don't have.

> As a musician, I corral a large number of component skills to accomplish tasks like performing, composing, or conducting. I need clear and accurate listening, theoretical knowledge, short- and long-term aural memory, physical technique, coordination, gestural clarity, and creativity, to name a few. Building each of these component skills by itself has required decades' worth of work, not to mention putting them all together.
>
> So, what happens when I turn around to teach music to others? I offer them the things I "have" in each of these categories, insights and experiences that help them see how professional musicians do what we do, what is required to develop those skills, and what may be helpful in facilitating their own training process. If I haven't experienced a component skill fully myself, I certainly cannot hope to pass it along effectively to my charges.

Let's try an example of this in, say, high school mathematics. A well-respected, highly successful algebra and geometry teacher is unexpectedly "asked" to teach one section of Business Math next fall. While she remembers a few of the core concepts from her undergraduate training, and has a great list of resources on hand, she hardly considers herself an expert in this particular subject matter. She quickly discovers that she has much less to give in comparison to her comfort courses in algebra and geometry. What to do?

A bit of creativity can go a long way in developing and expanding your own skill set to subsequently pass it along to students. Intense academic study and review could help our Business Math teacher as a start, but what real experiences might be available to her to provide better material for next semester? Can she shadow that CFO friend of hers for a couple weeks during the summer? Start her own simple small business, even a mock one, to actually put some principles into practice? Finally take up that longtime desire to dip her toe in online stock trading? Think of the difference in students' motivation in relation to a teacher who is obviously just staying one chapter ahead of them in the book, compared to a teacher who has engaged in real activities like these. Consider how these example experiences might apply to your own work in your field.

Teachers can increase and improve our subject matter wealth in small but powerful ways, all through paying attention to our environment and focusing our internal efforts. For instance, what additional insights can you gain about Physical Science while on recess blacktop duty? Deeper understanding of Language Arts during that guest speaker assembly? Discoveries about Geography while walking from your car to your classroom? Discover exactly what it is that you perhaps "don't have" right now, and challenge yourself to figure out how to get it. You may find that you don't need any materials, just life-changing experiences through careful observation and clear thinking. The good news about all of this, of course, is that you *can* give what you *do* have.

KEY IDEAS:

- Deeper mastery of your material can boost student engagement and achievement notably.
- A little observation and creativity can help us own our subject matter better.

GIVE EVERYTHING AWAY, RIGHT AWAY

We give students all sorts of things every day: our time, energy, ideas, creativity, support, sympathy, empathy, strategies, and solutions. Some days we may wonder "Do I have enough in the tank for everyone?" "Can I really keep up this pace?" and "Am I learning and growing sufficiently myself to offer students what they need?" In class, we may think of what we have to offer as a set, static storehouse of goods built over a long period of time. We can become a bit stale in the way we diagnose and treat the educational problems students bring us. "This is your challenge; here is the solution" can become rather mechanical and boring. Consider an antidote to the staleness itself: Give everything away, right away.

Hopefully, you continue to grow in your own understanding of your subject every day. You may find yourself imagining two similar but distant paths, your growth as a world historian and your students' growth in World History, or your growth as a poet and your students' growth in Creative Writing. It may seem that your path continues to extend gradually and infinitely, while your students' path resets year to year or semester to semester. After all, there is only so much that can be covered in that one year of British Literature or Art Appreciation.

When we look at curriculum as the *what* of learning, it is true that there is only so much we can explore in the limited time we have with our students. When we look at it as *how*, though, we may find rich opportunities to help them maximize their pace on the path. This is where giving everything away, right away can be helpful. Have you recently discovered a new online method of tracking personal diet that you could share with the Physical Education class tomorrow? A new trick for memorizing multiplication tables that your 8-year-old nephew (for goodness' sake!) just showed you after all these years of math expertise? An insight about Monet's stroke technique that you hadn't noticed before in all those trips to the city museum?

We may pass up the opportunity to share these findings right away because tomorrow's class is already planned, or it doesn't quite fit with the unit we are studying now, or it seems like it is something students should encounter later. Perhaps there is even a bit of pride or arrogance lurking in there: "This is an advanced concept, the kind of thing that *I'm* discovering; they are not ready for this yet." It is, of course, possible that students truly are not ready for a given concept, that it would make a lot more sense to introduce it later at a more opportune time. However, always consider the possibility that right now might just be the most opportune time.

Here's why. Students love to know that you are actively working in the field you teach. They respect your work as an art or literature teacher, but they love you as an artist or writer.

One morning I received one of those exceedingly rare face-to-face compliments from a high schooler: "Mr. B, you know why you and Mr. O [we all had one-letter nicknames] are such awesome teachers?" "Well . . . no, why?" "Because you actually DO what you teach." I was playing professional concerts regularly, and Mr. O, the science teacher, was developing a biofuel for our school district's buses. This student was viewing us not primarily as professional educators who had acquired a standard body of knowledge and skills just to pass it on to others, but as a musician and scientist who had chosen a lifetime of learning and teaching, receiving and giving.

I think I speak for Mr. O when I say that we took no great delight in sharing our learning in class as if it were big news. We simply recognized regularly the relevance between our own work and the lesson of the day, allowing our discoveries and the students' curriculum to blend and blur both in our internal thinking and our external interactions. Students' passion and motivation for the subject matter followed as a natural consequence.

A great reason to give everything away, right away is that it can create a fresh and spontaneous perspective on standard curricular concepts. On Monday morning, you may feel trapped by the necessity of covering a particular concept fully within limited class time, but if you go ahead and share what you learned over the weekend, the concept may get covered better anyway. Students will feel like they are learning something new and relevant because they *are* learning something new and relevant. As you tie it back into what they read or learned in preparation for class, they begin to see the relationships among various elements within the subject and perhaps even develop more respect for that old textbook or other learning resource.

Finally, giving everything away, right away serves as a valuable model for students. They see you making connections between your personal experiences and course content, and they learn to do the same. They see you presenting recent discoveries spontaneously, eloquently, and enthusiastically and they learn to do the same. And, perhaps most important, they see you giving freely and they learn to do the same.

KEY IDEAS:

- Your own newest discoveries in your field are likely the best you can offer.
- Be willing to break your routine; sharing spontaneous insights can inspire better learning.

IN A LEARNING SEQUENCE, JUST CHANGE ONE THING AT A TIME, TIME AFTER TIME

Think about it. Humans actually attend to only one thing at a time. When we are multitasking we are actually flipping back and forth very quickly between two or more activities. If school is to reflect "real life," we should set up learning sequences according to what humans naturally do. To maximize long-term progress, teachers can introduce, add, or change one thing at a time in a gradual succession of single steps.

The need for this suggestion arises from those moments when we pack in too many instructions at once. We may assume too much about students' prior knowledge, miscalculate their short-term memory potential, or simply try to beat the bell, causing us to quickly pile on several reminders and requirements simultaneously. The result is usually a sticky mess requiring much more time and energy than we would have used if we had approached it more methodically and patiently in the first place. Thinking it all the way through and guiding students along each step can ultimately build greater momentum and reduce backtracking.

Perhaps we should look closer at some of the reasons we pile on instructions. When we assume, for instance, that students know more than they do we may feel that we can fast-forward our communication and skip or combine steps of an activity. The challenge here is obviously knowing, or discovering, what students really do know already. We can ask them directly, distribute a short checklist or survey, or discuss it with current or previous teachers. In cases where there is no time or opportunity to probe, though, always consider erring on the side of academic safety when you start. It is much easier to begin a bit too basic and gradually accelerate as you discover students are readier than you imagined, than to start at a sprint only to lose most of the pack. Not only does the first approach provide an educational insurance policy, it also creates positive forward motion in students' minds as they start to stride.

We also might think students can remember multiple instructions as they tackle a task. Some of them can, sometimes, but this assumption can create substantial disappointment. Ask yourself, "Is it possible to break this down further?" If so, consider "Would it be ridiculous to do so?" If not, *break it down further*. Sometimes, of course, it would be ridiculous or even insulting to break down a concept further, but be sure to at least entertain the possibility. Some of this decision-making can be done prior to class; most of it happens in the moment. Either way, it can have a major influence on classroom pacing. Moving along can be exciting but also involves risk; calculate that risk wisely.

A final—and frequent—reason teachers pile on the instructions is when the bell is about to ring. We feel an urgent need to close out a complicated topic or fit in all of the homework instructions and we suddenly shift into a higher gear. This challenge is exacerbated by the fact that students' minds are starting to shift slightly (or fully) toward the next class or event in their day. The problem is two-fold: we begin talking faster and faster to students who are paying gradually less attention. We may think that students will hang on our every word because we know that the concept at hand is so crucial, but their minds may already be elsewhere.

How to solve this? Timing. You may need to simply delay a bit of the concept until next class, a move that can be quite helpful as students' minds dwell on unfinished business between meetings. Better yet, plan the timing meticulously beforehand and monitor it carefully, so that the bell cannot corner you.

Introducing, adding, or changing one thing at a time is helpful in and of itself, but the questions "Which thing?" "In what order?" and "Why?" remain. If we picture the proverbial journey of 1,000 miles, each step is important not only as a mathematical fraction of the overall distance but also in terms of its direction. If one could see the ideal trajectory of the journey in hindsight, and that the first step proceeded at a two-degree angle from it, that might make for one long trip. On the other hand, even if every step proceeds straight toward the goal, a rocky precipice or deep lake might stand in the way at some point. The wisest route probably involves some amount of curvature or zigzags and in each of these larger shapes, the individual steps may vary greatly. Some are simple, easy flat ones while others are high steps onto boulders. As teachers, our job is to see the big picture clearly. Then we can help students see what is coming and manage their smaller steps, changing one thing at a time, time after time.

KEY IDEAS:

- Breaking down concepts as reasonably far as possible can help students stay on track.
- Noticing when we tend to stack up instructions can help us plan better for next time.

STAY THREE STEPS AHEAD IN YOUR MIND, ONE STEP IN YOUR WORDS AND ACTIONS

Do you ever find yourself stuck in an unwanted pause in the classroom? A screeching halt or just a momentary blip caused by a memory lapse or unexpected event? Perhaps a transition between activities is taking longer than you hoped or you accidentally skipped a step and now you are scrambling to get everyone back on track. How can we cinch up, or eliminate altogether, these undesirable pauses? Staying three steps ahead in your mind, and one in your words and actions, is a slight internal shift that can yield substantial external results.

A disclaimer: this takes PRACTICE. Conceptual understanding of this strategy and even heartfelt agreement with it will not yield much of a change. What is required is gradually training your mind to be able to quickly hop back and forth between what students need in the moment and what they will likely need a few steps down the road. There are at least two factors working in your favor as you develop this skill: (1) you have the advantage already because you are the one that planned the lesson thoroughly (*if* you planned the lesson thoroughly!) and (2) you can practice this skill in all sorts of daily interactions, or even by yourself.

You probably already exercise this skill in personal exchanges; in fact, you must engage it to some extent to carry on a conversation coherently. It is what allows you to make logical, relevant responses to someone's questions or comments in a reasonable amount of time as you sit down to lunch. So, experiment with how far and wide you can stretch your mental space for that conversation as you engage in it. Do you detect a certain tone in your friend's voice that tips you off to what may be coming? Can you foresee your own likely response based on your personal history with that friend? Can you quickly choose a different response that may improve the outcome of the conversation and solve a problem or avoid a snag? This awareness of what is currently happening in front of you and how it relates to what might or should happen next is crucial to quality classroom interactions.

We all know that working with students, especially in large groups, can be highly challenging in the heat of the moment. We have planned today's material and sequenced the instructions and activities very carefully. We have set up the physical space for smooth transitions and forward momentum. The question remains: Are we ready to pace the day by attending to both the present exchange and the projected next steps in a constant forward mental flow? Can our minds follow two parallel paths simultaneously, the one we are observing and participating in and the one that should likely be happening in a few moments?

One might argue that because we cannot predict the future, projecting a few steps forward in our mind is useless. Or, perhaps that thinking ahead will cause us to miss something right now. It is true that we cannot predict what will happen next, so the "three steps ahead" path simply continues to evolve in our minds in tandem with the "here and now" path. Regarding the question of missing something right now . . . practice, practice, practice. You will soon find that you don't miss the present because the cycle between one step and three steps is constant and mutually reinforcing. In other words, keeping your eye on the next steps influences what you do or say in the present moment, which helps students keep moving in the right direction, which leads naturally to your vision of the next steps. Try it today in low-stress environments, perhaps even with a teacher friend who is in on the secret. You might be surprised at what you can do in there, in the privacy of your own mind. And thrilled at how it changes you in class.

KEY IDEAS:

- For ideal pacing, we should be able to balance present interactions with future steps.
- Spontaneously envisioning the pacing you hope to see takes lots of practice.

IN A LEARNING SEQUENCE, IF YOU CAN'T GO BACK, DON'T; IF YOU CAN, JUST DO IT

As our students progress through a series of small steps toward ultimate victory, we often find ourselves in a snag, wishing we could return to previous material. Perhaps students did not comprehend a step fully when we thought they had or maybe we accidentally skipped one altogether. Sometimes, we simply cannot go back due to time constraints, diminishing student interest, or differences in students' level of comprehension. We may have to choose another route or table the topic for another day when we can gather our thoughts and start over, perhaps with a new approach. At other times, we can actually backtrack and still maintain student engagement without losing momentum. If you find yourself in that situation, just do it.

What is suggested here is to avoid thinking aloud: "Oh, sorry, I missed a step there" or "Oh shoot, I messed that up. Now we have to go back and fix it." These sorts of statements are often accompanied by an air of frustration and additional self-directed comments. Totally unnecessary. Even though you may feel compelled to apologize and explain the situation, doing so simply slows things down. Assuming that you have created a fruitful educational environment in your room, your students just want to move on. So move on.

As an example, your science students may be creating an electromagnet with the basics—a metal rod, a hunk of wire, and a battery. You prepared all steps very carefully the night before, making sure that your overwhelming knowledge of how to successfully assemble the parts and understand how it works would translate clearly to students without assuming or overlooking any step. The students begin the project in pairs as you walk them through it and circulate among them. As they work, the gaps among their relative levels of completion spread more and more. Some of them wrap the wire easily and perfectly around the rod, always in the same direction, while others have a tough time even on multiple tries. As your attention becomes distracted by individual students' needs you quickly blurt "If your wire is wrapped perfectly (check it with your partner!) you may attach one end to each end of the battery with the electrical tape." The students who are ready for that step jump in eagerly, knowing they are almost done.

Problem: You forgot to tell them to strip the wire insulation first.

Electromagnets are not working. Faces fall. Questions begin. The moment of truth has arrived. What do you do? This may not sound like such a consequential decision but it can affect how classroom pacing proceeds and what students actually learn from this project. You are quick enough to recognize what went wrong. You know you have to get back to the stripping step with everyone on board. Do you begin apologies and explanations, sending the leaders backward and confusing those who have not yet arrived, or find a way to teach something to everyone?

A simple solution in this case, for instance, might be to challenge those who have almost finished to figure out why it did not work, and help the others to quickly reach the final step. Once everyone is at the same spot, the opportunity presents itself for a bit of class discussion. "What's missing (or extra)?" "Why do we need to strip it off to make this work?" and "Well then, why do they put insulation on wire in the first place?" Questions like these help students engage and apply the concepts better. Your mistake has actually prompted better learning.

We need not cover up our errors or maintain a false façade of perfection. Students should see us make mistakes and take responsibility for them, but not at the expense of their learning. Choose opportunities to admit your errors wisely. If students will benefit more from a creative save, keep those extraneous thoughts to yourself.

KEY IDEAS:

- Quick thinking in the moment of a misstep can offer unexpected learning opportunities.
- No matter the details of the situation, student growth is priority number one.

DON'T STATE THE OBVIOUS ANY MORE—*OR LESS*— THAN NECESSARY

Students like to be challenged. They like to move along. They like to make progress and improve their skills. Theoretically speaking, each student's path toward a given competency has an ideal pace. Practically speaking, that pace is generally unknown, to teachers and even to students themselves. A central factor in maintaining the best pace possible is monitoring and managing your communication of the obvious. If we state the obvious too often, we waste time, bore students, and even lose their trust. If we do not state it enough we may miss ripe opportunities to drive home an important point or trigger deeper understanding.

"The obvious" is a rather subjective term. Obvious to whom? How obvious? Obvious based on prior class discussions or truly common knowledge? Obvious from previous verbatim statements or obvious from other ideas that seem *to us* to lead to the current idea? Before we can determine whether or not to state the obvious, we must decide whether or not the content at hand actually is obvious.

As usual, this important decision typically presents itself with only a split second of time available, while twenty-five students are watching and waiting for your next move. You might sense very clearly that everyone in the room knows the answer to the question or has arrived at the logical conclusion. You could state it for everyone, or invite a volunteer to do so, but you would lose some momentum and disappoint your students, as they show expressions of "Yes . . . we *know*!" and "Can't we just move *on*?" This would be stating the obvious more than necessary.

Stating the obvious more than necessary results in students losing a bit of long-term engagement in your class with each instance of their wasted time and attention. Perhaps more crucial is that they start to automatically rely on you to state obvious conclusions rather than making those conclusions themselves. If they discover that you will always point the class gradually to an understanding, and then state it plainly for everyone, they are less likely to push toward that goal themselves on the next cycle. Instead, they will simply wait around, cognitively speaking, for you to deliver the goods.

A good substitute for stating the obvious unnecessarily is to leave an extra beat of silence. For example, someone has just asked a question demonstrating lack of understanding, you responded with a few guiding questions of your own, and the confusion has been tangibly cleared from the room. Instead of asking that student to reiterate the truth of the moment . . . again . . . let all of the students sit for a second with those light bulbs shining above their heads. We can enjoy the obvious together without stating it and it is much more satisfying when all of us have worked to reach it.

On the other hand, some situations beg for the obvious to be announced, and perhaps repeated. Probably, the most frequent example of stating the obvious *less* than necessary is when something seems readily apparent to the teacher, but not at all to the students. Unfortunately, there are many, many reasons why this can happen. For example,

- You have taught this material to other groups every year for several years.
- You have taught the same material today to another section of the class.
- You have been thinking like a sculptor, chemist, or historian for many years now.
- You have not explained a prerequisite concept as well as you thought you did.
- Your students did not attend to prior instruction as much as you thought they did.

These are just a few examples. In these cases, if and when the obvious eventually does get stated, it will serve as the moment of truth, revealing that it was not obvious at all to the students and perhaps pointing you to why. This can be conducive to improving the learning environment for the future.

Stating the obvious can be useful to students as a point of departure for the next concept. It helps everyone check in on the group's current status, so that all will be ready to proceed together. For example, you may be guiding students through a discussion of the storyline of a novel and arrive at a final, self-evident bit like "And when does the main character finally realize his mistake?" The obvious answer, to those who actually read the novel, is, "At the very end." If that is the final point in the whole unit, you might not want to force the middle schoolers to grunt the obvious on a Friday afternoon. However, if that point serves as a springboard to a discussion of creative writing techniques and conceptualizing a story from end to beginning, rather than beginning to end, then stating the obvious is a perfect opportunity to make the transition smoothly.

Finally, hearing what we already know stated in a different way can be quite enlightening. Just because the concept itself is obvious to students does not mean they have fully explored its ramifications. You have probably experienced this yourself. An old axiom, parable, fable, or cliché suddenly "spoke" to you in a completely different way as a 10-year-old, teenager, or young adult. You had heard it umpteen times before, but had never really internalized it like you did in that moment. Similarly, when we state the obvious in class, or encourage a student to do so, the meaning of the term or concept may suddenly reveal itself in a new way. We do not want to miss those opportunities for student discovery so we must remain vigilant. Fine tuning your obvious-radar is tricky business; just use your assumption-gauge and boredom-meter in tandem to guide you at every turn.

KEY IDEAS:

- A fine line separates obvious and not-so-obvious concepts in any given class.
- Upon deciding which is the case in the moment, teachers can use the obvious skillfully.

BETTER TO SAY SOMETHING ONE TIME MANY WAYS, THAN ONE WAY MANY TIMES

Most students have had a teacher or two along the way with a pet phrase or infamous declaration, something that was well known and perhaps frequently imitated. Some phrases may have been endearing, inspiring, or even educationally helpful. Others may have been downright annoying and aggravating. Teachers may also say the same thing several times in class for good reasons such as reinforcing a concept, clarifying a misunderstanding, or catching a few struggling students up with the rest of the group. Repeating oneself may seem like an effective, and justifiable, strategy but usually it is better to say something one time many ways, than one way many times.

In her sixth-grade math applications class, the teacher is reminding the students of the standard order of operations with the famous phrase "Please excuse my dear Aunt Sally." The "P" in "Please," of course, stands for "Parentheses," so that students will solve any operations within parentheses prior to folding that result into the rest of the equation. She has them repeat the mnemonic aloud, which is accompanied by more than a few passionate groans. She wonders if there might be other ways to characterize the concept of parentheses first, to reinforce this crucial concept for her students, and also avoid annoying them unnecessarily. What does Aunt Sally have to do with all of this anyway?

The teacher conjures up several ideas: parentheses serve as shelters from the rest of the equation until their tenants can finish their work; parentheses point outwards from the "top priority" operation of the equation; or parentheses look a bit like a partial circle, targeting the spot where your eyes should alight first.

In his elementary science class, the teacher is helping students understand why the sun always rises in the east. He attempts to keep hammering home the fact that the sun remains constant while the earth is rotating, that the sun is not really rising, but that the earth is turning toward it. Students accept this explanation at face value but are still struggling with the "rising in the east" part. The teacher realizes he is repeating himself but feels that his explanation is sufficient and true. The more he hammers, the less the students understand. He decides there must be a better way and discovers additional angles from which to clarify: physically manipulating a small globe spinning toward a clearly marked compass direction, and reviewing the gradual onset of light and darkness in various time zones across the country.

In her high school Economics class, the teacher notices that a few students seem to come up short on relatively simple topics. All of them are generally quite bright and known to be creative and open thinkers. She decides something is amiss and starts paying particular attention to their responses in class and on assignments. She begins to realize that the way she phrases instructions and descriptions are purposefully and meticulously aligned with the textbook, providing stellar consistency but cultivating sheer boredom. She resolves to seek different ways to phrase what the text and other course materials offer. For example, instead of simply parroting "The opportunity cost is the value sacrificed in the interest of an alternative acquisition or achievement," she finds herself saying things like "We all take risks; some of them are smart risks and others are just plain 'risky risks,' depending on how thoroughly we have considered what we might be leaving behind. The same is true in finance."

The parentheses, sunrise, and opportunity cost examples illustrate ways we can say things one time many ways, rather than one way many times. As the rotating globe example suggests, this approach is not strictly verbal but may involve all sorts of communication methods. However, verbalizations are a great place to start because we use them so frequently and they are relatively simple to self-evaluate. Start by giving yourself an initial checkup, asking pointed questions like: How many different ways can I express this concept? What are a dozen keywords related to this topic that I might draw on when I need to put it another way? What personal catch phrases can I set to trigger my internal alarm when I sense them about to roll off my tongue? What are some signals from students that my communication is getting a bit dull or predictable? How often do I allow myself to throw in a vocabulary word that might be just beyond their comfort zone but within their verbal reach? How might I use more colorful language and metaphors to make my points? How often do I break out of the character my students seem to have ascribed to me and give them a refreshing surprise communication? Is it possible to say *everything* I say only once, or at least close to it? Why not strive to make everything I say fresh and new? This is one small step for teachers, one giant leap for student engagement.

KEY IDEAS:

- A bit of self-assessment regarding repetitive verbalizations can go a long way.
- Devise numerous options for how you might communicate a given concept.

CHOOSE CAREFULLY WHICH THOUGHTS
TO PUT INTO WORDS

Some years ago, one of my undergraduates was peer teaching in a music educa-
tion course. She had just finished her work, and the customary peer feedback
followed. A fellow student said, "You know, at measure 42 you really didn't
have to say what you did," to which she quickly replied, "I know, I know, I'm
sorry, my mind just has no filter!" A description that, unfortunately, is all too
accurate too much of the time for teachers.

What, exactly, do we mean by a mental filter? In this case, she was referring
to something that crossed her mind, which could have simply dissipated by
itself, but which she chose to speak aloud. Instead of filtering the thought
away from her precious verbal space with the group, she let it speak up and
muddy the waters. If we can learn to observe our filtering process, we can
become more judicious about whether what crosses our mind really needs to
cross our students' minds.

The first step in this experimentation is simply observing your thoughts.
Where do they come from? When do they arise? What are their relative
strengths? Where do they go? To whom do they belong? For how long? What
determines whether they stick around? If you can slow things down enough
to focus internally for a few minutes, you can start to answer these questions
for yourself. The answers are unique to each of us. Do yourself the favor.

As we begin to notice how our thoughts operate, we also start to discover
that we can make decisions about them. We can choose to dismiss one
thought quickly and easily while entertaining another as very important for
quite a while. We can observe strings of thoughts and notice how they relate.
We can choose to cut off a given string or to shift it in a new direction, or
willfully entertain its polar opposite if only for the sake of experimentation.
Finally, we can decide what to do externally with those internal thoughts. Say
something? Take action? Make a change? Field a response? Offer an alternative? Improve a situation? These little realizations of our options for adjusting
and changing our thoughts, and translating them into external interactions, are
powerful moments.

Choosing which thoughts to put into words can be helpful in obvious situations like a confrontational parent meeting or a classroom management issue.
We may hold our tongue to let an antagonistic thought zoom by unspoken
or we may consciously choose to verbalize something that will save the day.
Subtler than these, however, are the constant choices we make about what to
express and how to express it during "normal" instruction. Monitoring our
thoughts and selectively expressing them can help us maintain a swift, appropriate pace, reduce confusing communication, avoid sequencing regrets, and

eliminate unnecessary tangents. Discover for yourself to what extent you have the power to choose which thoughts you put into words, and by all means exercise it.

KEY IDEAS:

- Exploring your thoughts and thought patterns regularly can help you focus them in class.
- What you say aloud truly is a choice; notice how it derives from your thoughts.

JUST THE RIGHT WORD IS BETTER THAN
DOZENS OF OTHERS

Words.

Beautiful little things, are they not? Dangerous too. A single word in class has the power to turn on the proverbial light bulb, fuel the proverbial fire, move the proverbial mountain . . . and to slam on the proverbial brakes. Chances are you use quite a few words throughout the school day, in class and out. Choosing just the right one in a given moment can make all the difference in how that day goes.

We all have experienced a point in conversation when we cannot find the word we need. Often, people will even say, "Hmmm . . . what's the word I'm looking for?" before remembering it either on the spot or 30 minutes later when the conversation is long over. In the moment of struggle we hem and haw, thinking through alternatives, words that sound similar but have nothing to do with the topic, and even asking those around us for help. Why are we so intent on finding that specific word? Perhaps because we need to prove to ourselves our memory is not failing, perhaps because it really annoys us in the moment, but mostly because it is *just the right word*. There is a tangible feeling that that word will save the day.

In class the effect just described is multiplied by the number of students. Perhaps twenty-five to thirty-five—or more—eager people are hanging on that single word. And we want to deliver. This may be starting to sound a bit dramatic, but the truth is that it really matters. Pinpointing just the right word at just the right time helps us drive home an important point accurately. Nothing else will do. If we stumble around for a bit, try some other words, and attempt to patch up the concept, we can generate at the very least a half-baked idea or connection, and at most a mountain of misunderstanding. It can take a lot more words to help students get back on track.

What are some ways we can avoid or conquer the "What's that word?" trap? Stop talking. Instead of thinking aloud, verbally buying some time, leave a moment of silence to *truly* focus on the needed word. A single second of really clear mind can work wonders. The added benefit to this approach is that students get to use that moment of silence too, to process what you have just been saying and where you might be going. In fact, they may even think of the word themselves without your requesting it. After all, we all probably also have been in conversations where we pitched in just the right word for our friend who needed it. It requires a certain amount of attentiveness and engagement to do this, factors we just so happen to hope our students are bringing to class.

That being the case, another approach to the trap might be asking aloud in class "What's that word I'm looking for?" Students love competition and they love to know something the teacher doesn't know, if only for a fleeting moment. Let them have the double satisfaction, and save the day to boot. They may also start to predict where you are going with concepts in the future more readily, and nothing improves pacing more than a teacher and students staying on the same page on a regular basis.

Most of this description has been a defensive position—how to avoid getting stuck and how to survive while finding your way out. Consider also the power of choosing just the right word for bonus points. For example, is there a vocabulary word that you are pretty sure students do not know, but that inserted in context of what you just described in class will teach it to them effortlessly? Use that word instead of the one they already know. Is there a bit of metaphoric language you could layer in that would challenge students to connect a concept in a new way and therefore reinforce it even more? Is there a word that is simply rarely used, but that fits perfectly and will spark, or reignite, their attention?

I recently had the delightful opportunity of reminding students, once again, that we were approaching the absolute final deadline for turning in an assignment. Just as I was about to use the same old boring language to beat the poor horse one last time, a fresh word came to mind for no apparent reason: "If I haven't heard from you yet on this assignment, be sure to submit it forthwith." I saw them reeling for a split second as they processed the surprise word, so I followed up to finish the one-two punch: "And when I say forthwith, I mean posthaste." Eyes darted back and forth for a moment; then wide grins gradually emerged. And the papers came in.

Have some fun with words. Choose just the right one to make a point, widen students' vocabulary, or spark and maintain their engagement. Students will be more likely to maintain interest in what you say if they can expect to discover a gem on occasion. More important, your love of words may just rub off on them. You may find that they are more able and willing to use specific words effectively in class if you have set an example.

KEY IDEAS:

- Finding that perfect word is worth the trouble, and can bring surprising benefits.
- Cultivate a love of words in your room; students grow into their environment.

AN EXAMPLE IS WORTH A THOUSAND WORDS

Do you ever find yourself struggling to explain a concept to the class? Like *why* two negative numbers yield a positive number when multiplied or *how* to confidently determine the difference between direct and indirect objects? Furthermore, *why* either of these is the slightest bit important to students' futures? Your best bet in answering any of these questions may be finding just the right example, ultimately saving you unnecessary, and perhaps problematic, words.

Finding just the right example may, and should, imply choosing from many options. A teacher might think of three or four examples of how two negatives become a positive and choose the one that fits the students' gap in understanding perfectly on a given day. Or, perhaps that same teacher will exhaust all three or four of those options to reach different students in the class on a tougher day. Naturally, the quality of example you choose depends on the number and caliber of examples you have explored in preparing the concept for instruction.

Why do examples work so well in teaching? They seem to be our most natural way of learning. In daily life, as young children, we field lots and lots of examples of events, responses, interactions, sequences, and consequences, and gradually form concepts about the way the world works: deductive reasoning at its best. In school, teachers often put the cart before the horse by presenting the deduction as an accepted truth and then following up with an example only when required, requested, or convenient.

Verbalizing terms and concepts allows us to communicate knowledge efficiently and effectively, summing up a great deal of time-consuming experiences in a moment of spoken word. However, we might appeal to students' natural discovery mode and generate longer-lasting learning if we offer them examples that prompt them to recognize a truth gradually and organically instead.

Pay attention to the examples you discover for yourself that may help you grasp your area of expertise more fully, and log the best ones for future use. Try to have a handful of examples at the ready for each major concept you will cover in class, especially those that seem to be perennially elusive. Get in the habit of presenting a variety of high-quality examples first, and guiding concept discovery second. Choose examples wisely from a number of options depending on the students' particular needs in the moment when problems arise. And, finally, encourage students to generate lots of examples themselves. If they learn by examples, discover a truth, and then create their own examples, they will have mastered concepts thoroughly, tied them to unforgettable applications, and saved a lot of confusing verbiage along the way.

KEY IDEAS:

- Examples are a natural route to deductive reasoning and lasting learning.
- Teachers can use their own experience with examples to guide their use of them in class.

MODELING IS A POWERFUL TOOL

For better or for worse.
 Use it wisely.

> *As I watched the 8-year-olds in basketball practice, I was impressed with how the assistant coach was inspiring such a high level of positive energy, motivation, and forward momentum. At present, the boys were in line taking short-range jump shots in quick succession. The coach and other players would catch any stray rebounds and pass them right back to the shooter to get back to the end of the line quickly. One shooter made a playful, innocuous comment that he was "hitting everything, even better than Coach!" His next shot careened sideways off the rim right toward this assistant coach, who caught it with one hand, faked a pass back to the kid, and rolled it in an equally playful and innocuous manner to the other corner of the gym. No harm done, all in good fun, but it was all over.*
>
> *You know what happened next, right? I've never seen so many boys rolling stray rebounds to the four corners of a gym. It was a chance to put someone else behind in the rotation. A chance to fake someone out. A chance to be funny.*
> *A chance to imitate the coach.*
>
> *The rhythm of the activity disintegrated. Pacing vanished. Focus and motivation shifted completely. Forward momentum was nowhere to be found. As I began to wonder how the engineer was going to get the train back on its tracks, the head coach whistled for all groups to circle up. The activity was over.*

This bout of mild chaos was a rare occurrence for the assistant coach, which may be why it was so striking. Modeling something—anything—can be a powerful form of communication to others. In this example, it affected a specific behavior within the activity, not exactly related to the game of basketball. Similarly, in our classrooms students may exhibit behaviors seemingly "apart" from the course content. Note, however, that the change in peripheral behaviors also slowed the pace of basketball skill development.

Modeling can play a direct role in the core content of our subject matter. In teacher training and lesson planning, modeling is often thought of as something to do *first*: The teacher models how to solve the quadratic equation and then the students try it themselves under her supervision. Often, however, the most powerful models happen in the moment, *after* students have attempted something, to help them see how they could alter and improve it the next time around. The students try the quadratic equation, miss a step, and produce the wrong answer. The teacher then puts the equation on the screen and walks them through the pitfalls. These models are powerful because students are ideally primed for learning. They have found themselves in a tight spot and have a genuine desire to discover what they need to get out.

These after-models can be a bit frightening because we cannot prepare for them. They are not only spontaneous, responsive, and compassionate but also potentially treacherous. Like any teaching skill, responsive modeling becomes more familiar and more comfortable the more we use it. Observing students' actions clearly gives us the best chance at responding appropriately and maintaining forward motion.

The purpose of observing and improving our own modeling is not to simply avoid making mistakes, or to somehow perfect it for future use. We will mess it up sometimes, and that can produce some of the most thorough learning of all. Control the modeling factors you can control, remain vigilant and conscientious about your preparation for those difficult moments, and be prepared to mess it up once in a while. As you recognize your own mistakes in front of the class, and take the time to correct them and continue on, you will be modeling that too. The best teachers pay close attention to how well their models are functioning across all aspects of instruction, both planned and spontaneous. They note the effects their models may have had, and consider how to polish them for future use. I bet that assistant coach did.

KEY IDEAS:

- Modeling is a powerful form of conveying ideas, skills, and attitudes.
- Teachers can use modeling not only to pave the road but also to fix the potholes.

PREPARE YOUR FIRST MOVE IN A LESSON CAREFULLY; IT IS THE ONLY ONE YOU CAN PREDICT

Teaching is full of surprises. Intercom announcements, fire drills, and individual student "emergencies" can easily interrupt the flow of a class and send it in a new direction. Experienced teachers learn to expect the unexpected and to get the train quickly back on its tracks, but nobody can learn to predict when, exactly, surprises will arrive. Since you never know how class will proceed once it has begun, be sure to prepare at least your first words or actions of a lesson carefully; they are the only ones you can predict.

Many teachers overlook the importance of that first move they make in a class meeting. They have a clear sense of direction for the day, with the main landmarks of their lesson plan firmly established. However, they may be taking for granted that students will find their way into small groups quickly, or successfully review the last principle learned yesterday, or remember the steps they should complete in their application projects. Be sure that your very first verbal instructions, demonstration, or physical gestures are prepared clearly so that students get off to a great start.

This tends to be one of the most common self-realizations for student teachers: "I know I got off to a slow start in this lesson; I hadn't actually thought about *how* students would get into place quickly [or how, exactly, I would verbalize the rules of the activity, or when, exactly, I would tell them to pair up]." Even without any surprises or interruptions like a fire alarm or assembly announcement, notice how a class like this could turn out to be quite challenging.

Classroom surprises do not always arrive in tangible packages either. A surprise might simply be an unexpected student question, a general lack of understanding by the whole group, or an unforeseen readiness to move forward more quickly. We cannot predict these subtle timing issues but we can predict, well in advance, the very first move we will make based on the last meeting we had with those students.

Backwards planning is a wonderful pedagogical concept that encourages us to lay out our lessons with the end in mind. We ask ourselves where we see students at the finish of a given period of instruction, how we will get them there according to major milestones, and how we might sequence smaller bits of instruction to pass each of those milestones appropriately along the way. One potential challenge in planning this way is that the very first moments of a class meeting might naturally become the last thing entered in the plan, either physically in a document or mentally in our conception. We must make sure that we follow through all the way to the end (beginning) of the line, so that the start of the lesson is a great one.

Getting off to a great beginning is helpful, of course, even when things go as planned. Just as putting a bit of money into an interest-yielding account *right now* is the best way to build some financial momentum, planning those first words or actions for the very beginning of class is the best way to build pedagogical momentum. In the long term, as students start to know you as a teacher who kick-starts class effectively, they learn to treat your room as a fruitful, productive, efficient place where things get done and much is expected of them. In an environment like that, when surprises present themselves, both teacher and students will be more prone to get back to forward momentum as soon as possible. By all means, plan your whole next lesson thoroughly, but pay a bit of special attention today to how it will *start* tomorrow.

KEY IDEAS:

- Surprises abound in classrooms; we should meticulously plan a great start every day.
- Effective first moves can prompt class momentum and better student engagement.

WHAT YOU DON'T SAY IS AS IMPORTANT
AS WHAT YOU DO SAY

Maybe more!

We tend to talk a lot in the classroom, evidenced by some teachers losing their voice periodically and others simply being exhausted at the end of the day. Why do we do it? To get our point across, to make sure everyone understands, to reinforce essential information. Weaker and more honest reasons might be that we love to entertain our students, that our speaking helps maintain classroom control, or that perhaps we are just enamored with the sound of our own voice. No matter how noble our reasons for teacher talk may be the things we say can easily get in the way. Sometimes, we can help students best through a conscious decision to hold our tongue.

A primary reason for doing so is that every time we speak we run the risk of putting words in students' mouths. This old phrase really means "planting ideas in students' heads" or, more broadly and brutally stated, doing some of our students' thinking for them. Ouch! Viewed this way, our speaking could sometimes be undermining what we desire most for our students, like bright and original ideas, independent learning skills, and self-efficacy.

For example, teacher questioning can be used to reinforce the steps a student should take to learn a concept or procedure successfully.

- "Well, how are you going to get x by itself in this [algebraic] equation?"
- "What has to happen for those clouds to produce rain in the first place?"
- "And then . . . how do you modify this [Italian] adjective to make it align with the noun in gender and number?

We may ask these sorts of questions to the whole class or to individuals as we canvas the room, hoping they will learn eventually to ask themselves in like manner. The job is not finished, though, until you cease to ask the questions. Students may respond by requesting your assistance or giving you quizzical and helpless looks, but the time has arrived for you to leave a bit of open space. Chances are the appropriate question will arise within them if it has been prepared well and given the chance. By not saying anything, or by responding with simply "Mmm hmmm . . ." or "Well . . ." you put the onus on students to do the thinking.

Another big reason to hold your tongue from time to time is to provide a break in the cognitive action. Every little thing we say in class is something more for students to field. Extra. In addition. On top of. Is what you are about to say really necessary? Does it contribute cleanly and clearly? Would class be just as good, or maybe better, if you kept quiet for a moment instead?

We often use the phrase "digesting information" to compare perception and assimilation during learning to the act of eating. In both, students need repeated mini-cycles of receiving and processing, receiving and processing, to accomplish the task successfully. They need frequent small windows of opportunity to absorb the things you are saying, and you are the one that can afford them those moments. In music, the silences make the sounds stand out much more effectively. When you teach, what you don't say may be as important as what you do say. Use both with purpose.

KEY IDEAS:

- Too much teacher talk can rob students of thinking opportunities.
- Providing small breaks in the stream of verbalization helps students absorb the material.

THE TOUGHER TASK IS NOT TO DECIDE WHAT TO PUT IN, BUT WHAT TO LEAVE OUT, OF A CLASS

Our teacher brains are stuffed with expertise, an abundance of knowledge, skills, and experience that we are eager to share with students. We pounce on next term's courses with a general blueprint of overarching goals and outcomes. Then comes the real planning, determining how to allot the time we have to make satisfactory progress day by day. We have so much to offer them so it is usually more difficult to decide what to leave out of a class, than what to put in it.

All of that expertise has to be shared gradually in a logical, sequential fashion for students to grasp it best. It is not uncommon to hear a teacher or speaker say, "I could go on for hours about this, but . . ." and they probably could. Due to time constraints, or perhaps potential irrelevance, they decide for the better and move on toward the goal for the day. Sometimes, this is a difficult decision because golden learning opportunities often arrive unexpectedly.

During preparation, we have to make fairly firm decisions about what really belongs in class tomorrow and what, by necessity, must wait for another day—or perhaps never even arise. We know that we could lead students in several directions and extend their learning significantly in each, but we simply cannot or should not do it. We may be at the mercy of time, or we realize there are more crucial concepts, or we know that those additional ideas will be covered next year in someone else's class. For many of us, it requires a good deal of self-restraint to resist the appeal of diving in deeper and exploring more.

During class, the decisions become even trickier. We often face the choice of capitalizing spontaneously on an auspicious moment or knowingly passing it by, for instance. Either decision yields unique benefits depending on the situation. Obviously, we cannot always stick to the plan and ignore a prime opportunity, but we must be judicious as we respond to the moment. Is the content in question really crucial or just attractive? Will it derail the class for a long while or just a couple of minutes? Is it possible to acknowledge it briefly, providing a "teaser" for what is to come later in the unit? Or, acknowledge it clearly and openly as something that will be explored in more depth next year? Could we invite those who wish to hear more about it to come by during flex period or the end of lunch? The good news about appraising the situation with questions like these is that your decision does not have to boil down to a single "Yes, put this in" or "No, leave this out."

Be creative about how you determine what to leave out of a lesson, both during the comfort of pre-planning and the hailstorm of classroom decision-making. We all probably experience those moments when we wish we could "go on for hours" but we must keep the big picture in sight. Remind yourself of your *highest* priorities for your students regularly. Check and recheck how your content and activities align with those priorities, and plan to leave out those things that do not quite make the cut. Be tough on yourself about weeding out extraneous material. That will leave more room for what really matters and keep the learning running smooth.

KEY IDEAS:

- Explore good reasons for leaving something out of a given lesson plan; you decide.
- Maintaining a clear sense of overall purpose will aid you in those decisions.

BE READY WITH A REASON

If we want to encourage critical thinking in our students, by pressing them to ask "Why?" frequently (see earlier essay on page 67), then we should be ready with a reason whenever possible. Nobody in his right mind enjoys going along with a project or activity without knowing its purpose. Formal education is especially prone to this potential problem because some of what students do in our classes is at least one step removed from practical scenarios. We are teaching them *how to think*, not just how to solve specific problems.

The fact that "teaching" thinking sometimes requires a measure of distance from practicality should drive us more urgently to clarify our rationale for the activities we prescribe. Students need to know why one part of a project is necessary for the rest, why this bit of information is needed for that, why it is useful to do the whole thing over again from the very beginning, or why the professionals and experts choose to do it the way they do. If you have encouraged critical thinkers, you should be fielding the question "Why?" frequently throughout the day. Students may be asking the question to you directly or asking you to speculate on someone else's behalf.

In all cases, be ready with a reason. It is one thing to gradually stagger into a response when you are on the spot, quite another to reply swiftly and confidently, showing that you have already thought things through with students' best interests in mind. This can help students recognize that considering the reasons for doing something is the key counterpart to asking why they are doing it. You can help them round out both sides of their critical inquiry.

Being ready with a reason also benefits you internally, serving as a check on your own motives and view of the big picture. Students' long-term growth depends on your clear conception of why they are taking each step, step by step, in a learning sequence. If you are ready enough with a reason such that you could express it to someone else at a moment's notice, you have obviously clarified and reinforced it for yourself, ultimately contributing positively to students' experience in your room.

Being ready with a reason does not mean you have to blurt it out every time it is summoned. You might have a rationale crystal clear in your own mind but choose to disseminate that information systematically, gradually, or creatively, to ultimately help students see the magic plan even more fully. A great way to engage their critical thinking is to answer a "Why?" question with a specific set of circumstances under which they will no doubt discover the answer (e.g., by the end of the second phase of the project, when they get their test back, by Friday's class). This type of response not only reassures them that there is, indeed, a good reason but also could spark additional contemplation on their part in the interim.

Finally, we must consider whether there really should be a good reason for everything we do in school. One might argue that many things we do in "real life" are not very rational or logical, and they still work out splendidly. We can explore those possibilities with our students too, even when we do actually have a reason for it. Examples could be "It's good to be spontaneous sometimes," "It's okay to try a new way that has never been tested," "It's healthy to make a change once in a while just for the sake of fresh air," or "Some of the most innovative ideas come from abandoning the logic of the past." These can be great reasons too; committing to them and calling on them when students ask might just improve their thinking dramatically.

KEY IDEAS:

- Having good reasons ready for what we do in class helps us meet students' needs better.
- The more confident your rationale, the more you can enjoy students' probing questions.

THE FASTER YOU CAN DIAGNOSE A LACK OF UNDERSTANDING, THE BETTER THE INSTRUCTION

This statement may sound obvious at first, but pay attention to the keyword: diagnose. Most teachers are skilled at identifying *symptoms* of students' misunderstanding: an incorrect test answer, an irrelevant question during discussion, a missed step in the procedures. Students' peers are also quite adept at noticing these mistakes and even pointing them out publicly. The real challenge, with the big payoff, is determining the *cause* of the misunderstanding as quickly as possible.

Consider a class of fourth-grade math students working on a word problem that requires them to add up three legs of a long road trip and convert the total from miles to kilometers. Raised hands trickle in slowly at first and then flood the room. The teacher invites responses and their answers vary widely. Some students have obviously misunderstood one step or another. What caused it?

In a scenario like this, the teacher may already have some estimates of incorrect answers in mind based on one potentially missed step or another. For example, if students sum the distances correctly, but mistakenly use the conversion factor for kilometers to miles instead of miles to kilometers, the teacher may recognize it immediately based on their answer. At that point, it may seem like the teacher's job is finished, but the real diagnosing still remains. Why, or how, did the student use the wrong conversion factor? Lazy? Misread the summary conversion factor chart? Typed it in incorrectly? Did it by (faulty) memory to save time? Copied from a neighbor? Copied from a lightly penciled answer by last year's student in the same book? *These* questions can make the extra time you take to observe your students worthwhile. In far too many instructional interactions, a lot of time and energy is expended only to discover that a simple, irrelevant factor actually caused the original problem.

Let us assume, though, that the trouble presented in the scenario above was caused by a true conceptual misunderstanding. How might a teacher diagnose it quickly and effectively? Doctors use many methods to diagnose illnesses, but usually their first line of defense is directing a few logically ordered questions to the patient. This not only yields basic information describing the problem but also allows the doctor to pick up on clues inherent in the way the patient responds (shortness of breath, pained facial expression, raspy voice, sagging cheek, or slight shivering, for example). We can do the same in the classroom to help us determine what students are missing. What do their responses to our probing questions point up about relative confidence and mastery of each step?

Diagnostic questions might be asked to the whole class, to one student in the midst of the class, or to individual students or small working groups in isolation, depending on the instructional objectives for the day. If the word problem above was used for review, then asking the whole class why certain incorrect answers arose might help everyone reaffirm the rules of thumb for themselves prior to tomorrow's test. Note that asking the whole class why or how the *correct* answer arose is also helpful. If word problems are being used for differentiated learning, though, then rotating among small groups of students and asking diagnostic questions in private may be the way to go.

The main point is to be highly observant, pick up on all the clues, and go deep to the heart of the problem as quickly as possible. Telling a student "You converted from kilometers to miles" is like telling a patient "Your shoulder is hurting." They need you to help them figure out why and to nip the problem in the bud for the future. Perhaps, for example, students need to realize and remember that answers in kilometers are always larger than answers in miles from which they were converted. Some students may need to create their own conversion chart layout so that the relationship of the two measurements is bulletproof for them. Others may need to reverse-check their conversions to ensure they typed in the original numbers carefully and correctly.

There are several good reasons to improve your diagnostic speed. Doing so can give you options for how you will shape your next round of questions to help students take full advantage of a learning opportunity. Somewhat in contrast to the doctor, the teacher's job is not just to discover and state the diagnosis and proposed solution but also to guide the *students* to do so. If you can figure things out quickly, you have a much better chance of asking wisely chosen follow-up questions to prompt their own thinking.

Quickening your diagnosis skills also helps in class discussions. When a student asks a question or makes a comment that misses the mark completely, the quality of your response depends on the extent to which you understand *how* the student got off track. Again, a lot of time and trouble can be saved if you can respond directly to the *cause* of the misunderstanding rather than the symptoms. Finally, quick diagnosis may help you clarify instructions for the whole class based on what you discovered from one or a few students. For example, careful attention to *why* the first student who ran the obstacle course in Physical Education missed the rock climb completely might prompt you to tweak the layout or the instructions for everyone else—simple stuff, but always worth a second look.

KEY IDEAS:

- Diagnosing a misunderstanding may require prediction, keen observation, and tact.
- Increasing our diagnostic quickness improves the quality of interactions with students.

IF YOU SPELL IT ALL OUT, NOBODY GROWS

Ponder the phrase "spell it all out." We use it a lot, but what does it actually imply? If we literally spell something out for others, we give them the smallest possible bits of information, stripping the material down to bulletproof communication. We do this, for example, to make sure that someone on the other side of the counter or the other end of the phone conversation records our last name exactly as it is. These small details can cause a lot of trouble if errors are embedded.

"Spelling it out" has many metaphorical uses as well, generally implying a similar breakdown and transfer of material, piece by piece, to our audience. In classrooms, this can be very effective for communicating crystal-clear instructions or helping students through activities that require task analysis. However, in many cases spelling it all out inhibits students' growth.

Micromanaging students' learning makes it far less likely they will make inferences. Students need opportunities to make leaps forward, to experience what it feels like to go from A to C, not always A to B to C. If you carefully and considerately lay out A, B, and C for them, students will thank you for it in the moment. However, if you lay out A and C and help them figure out B, or how to get to C without it, they will thank you for it later. Students often do not realize at the time how lucky they are that a teacher is making them work hard for something, but down-the-road gratitude is usually sweetest.

The first question to contemplate would be what actually constitutes spelling it out in a given situation. "Is what I am about to do too explicit, too detailed, or too generous?" The answer to this arrives on a case-by-case basis, and only by your expert judgment of your particular students' progress. *Do* ask the question, though, and ask it frequently.

One clear indicator to help us decide is the second part of the original observation, "nobody grows." Pay close attention to your students' behaviors and responses as they progress through a new concept or practice a new skill. Are they breezing through in a somewhat robotic manner, repeating to themselves under their breath the academic mantra you gave them for the day? Are they frequently asking you for reminders of things they should be able to recall logically or systematically for themselves? Do they exhibit occasional glazed-over facial expressions and off-task behavior? If so, perhaps they need a challenge. They are not being encouraged, or required, to grow.

On the other hand, students who *are* growing tend to exhibit behaviors like trial-and-error, erasures, discussion among themselves, checking work with a voluntary partner, or questions to the teacher like "Couldn't you also do it this way?" or "Why not this first, and then that?" These extension questions show they are thinking critically about the material at hand, most likely born of their habituation to taking small (or large) leaps for themselves.

We probably all prefer the student behaviors in the second description, so why do we fall into the trap of spelling it all out? Lots of reasons. Perhaps we do not want to have to repeat ourselves, or to confuse students, so we communicate very clearly and explicitly the very first time we approach a topic. Maybe we have very little time to cover a unit or concept so we revert to efficiency as top priority. We may have encountered student confusion on the current topic in previous years, and decide to obey our clarity radar. Perhaps we want to make sure every single student is grasping the concept quickly so we cannot afford to leave much unsaid. We might feel that we have really thought the concept through so well that no better way of approaching it is possible. Any of these reasons may be valid for a given topic on a given day, but all of them lead to spelling it out and, sometimes, reduced student growth.

One of the important distinctions we can make is between the clarity of our practical instructions and the extent of our content contributions. We certainly do not want to leave out a crucial piece of procedural information as we set students up to get to group work, but we may choose to leave out a piece of *conceptual* information on purpose to lead the groups to growth. For instance, a teacher might make absolutely sure students have their graph paper rotated correctly, and protractor positioned appropriately, but purposefully choose not to tell them how to find those numbers they need. The teacher has been clear about the practical matters, to avoid unnecessary regrets, but has left the target thinking to the students.

Creating extra space in class for students to make their own leaps can be scary business, but usually this small investment of instructional time pays big dividends. Students can be physically arranged to keep each other on the same page as they make discoveries. That way, not only do they learn to teach each other, they also have the opportunity to witness others making inferences. Finally, if we think we have already discovered the "ultimate" way to introduce and reinforce a new concept ourselves, we may be reluctant to have students scuff up the polish on our planned pedagogy. This bit of pride probably just needs to go away; let the students wrestle with the content themselves instead to help them learn how to learn. *Well* worth the trouble.

KEY IDEAS:

- Clarity is helpful, but too much detail can stunt students' growth.
- We can spell out the practical matters of an activity without giving away the goods.

BEING SNEAKY IS FINE—PREFERABLE, EVEN—IF YOUR STUDENTS WILL LEARN BETTER AS A RESULT

I probably run a risk with readers on this one. People generally have an automatic aversion to sneakiness, especially if it may involve tricking unsuspecting students. Let me clarify with two examples.

I once was teaching an adult how to play a complicated drumset beat requiring coordination of both hands and both feet. The target pattern was a natural extension of some previous patterns he had mastered, but for some reason he was having a lot of trouble with this one. I modeled various layers of the beat on my drumset and he copied them on his, but the overall coordination just wasn't there. Instead of trying yet another angle, or describing it anew, or giving a bit more pep talk, I said, "Let's just leave that one for a few minutes and play something else to take your mind off it." He readily agreed.

He thought we were going to shift gears completely; I knew we were going to build that pattern from the ground up, tiny bit by tiny bit, at an unrecognizably slow musical pace. As he gradually progressed, mimicking my every move, I purposefully added the layers of complexity in an order that kept the infamous final pattern a secret until the very end. I somehow managed to keep my poker face as he added layer upon layer of the once impossible pattern, until suddenly he was playing the whole thing. I may have been as surprised as he was when he stopped short and said, "Nate, I believe you just tricked me into playing that beat [huge grin]." He was right.

In a very different scenario, but a related example, I once was having trouble getting my high school Spanish I students to pronounce their new vocabulary words well. They repeated them after me, and after recordings, and after guest lecturers. They played games and had contests, but the pronunciation was not improving much. As with the drumset player, I began to sense diminishing returns. I also knew, from years of teaching and tutoring language, that poor pronunciation often leads to low motivation for subsequent learning. We left the pronunciation activities for the day and moved to something else.

Before the next morning, I pondered the problem and realized that the main trouble was the vowel sounds. Students were managing the consonant combinations fine, but the vowels fell flat, reverting back to a more guttural American English accent. The next morning, the first thing we did after homework checks was a "sound memory game," where they had to remember and repeat sequences of sounds in two competitive teams. The students didn't realize that all of the target sounds were Spanish vowels in the sequential combinations in which they appeared in their vocabulary words (e.g., "ee-oo-oh" corresponding to "tiburón"). And I wasn't about to tell them. They thought it was a memory game for prizes; I knew (or hoped) it was a backdoor entrance to dramatically

improved pronunciation. Sure enough, when we finished the exercise, we fol-
lowed up by reviewing each vowel sound sequence and its corresponding word
in pairs. Amazing difference. Again, the students realized they had been duped,
but happily so.

These examples point up a few important factors to consider as you sharpen
your teaching stealth. Being sneaky can happen in the moment, if you are
open-minded and willing to try, or it can be planned ahead of time, depending on students' needs. Most teachers probably do not want to lie to students,
so don't. Just don't tell them what you are doing next when appropriate, and
allow it to unfold naturally.

Also consider the possibility of *starting* a given class period with the
trickery, as in the Spanish I example. Students are usually freshest, and least
suspicious, at the very beginning of class. They may have forgotten where
you left off last class, so your chances of easing them into a concept are probably much higher. When all those faces are beaming, you'll realize that being
"sneaky" is not such a bad thing at all.

KEY IDEAS:

- Taking students' minds off of a challenge can ultimately help them conquer it.
- Sneaky assistance can happen in the moment or as part of your plan; use
  both.

DO THINGS THE HARD WAY FROM TIME TO TIME

Human beings are quite enamored with efficiency. If there is a quicker more direct way to accomplish something, with the same high-quality results, we will choose that way every time. Discoveries and technological tools help us do things the easy way, rightfully capitalizing on the progress of the past and making the most of opportunities in the present. The new, easier way works just as well as the old way so we lose absolutely nothing in the process—except maybe a chance for growth. In daily life and in education, doing something the hard way from time to time can generate benefits far greater than the stated goal of the activity.

Examples abound of choosing between the hard or easy way in everyday tasks. Should I walk the half mile to the store to pick up a few small items for dinner or take the car? Ride the elevator up those two stories to my place or take to the stairs? Reach for my phone to make that three-digit calculation or use my brain? Trust my GPS navigation completely or take a good look at the whole route to make sure it makes sense? Although these decisions depend on a number of practical factors in the moment of making them, doing things the hard way can provide bonus benefits when feasible. Either way, you will get that dinner, arrive at your place, complete the calculation, or get to your destination. By doing each the hard way, though, you might also get some fresh air and save some gas, exercise your body, use your mathematical mind, and reinforce your sense of direction and geography, respectively. Taking the hard way becomes a small investment in yourself to complement the tangible results you could have enjoyed either way.

The same principle applies in education. Students frequently encounter a choice between carrying out some function themselves or relying on a tool to get the answer or solve the challenge quickly and easily. Too often, this choice is absolutely automatic: Get the tool and get it done. We certainly should take the easy way most of the time. Failure to use the tools we have at our disposal would be silly. However, providing occasional opportunities for students to take the hard way can be a big boost to their learning for several reasons.

First, students might develop their bodies and minds in basic but crucial ways. For example, they might work in groups to move tables or benches back into place quickly and cleanly rather than leaving them for the janitor to do with the machine. What do they gain? Muscular development, coordination, teamwork skills, distance estimation skills, and the satisfaction of helping out. They might draw a basic map of their community from memory for use on a project rather than printing one online. What do they gain?

Strength of imagination, spatial relationship skills, and working memory for relevant details.

Second, students have a better chance of seeing the big picture in a given situation. For example, students can retrieve an important name, date, or place from the Internet in an instant, but the very nature of that retrieval betrays the way they likely use it—as a simple bit of information, isolated from all the rest, and likely to require similar retrieval in the future. How much more beneficial would it be to forego the specificity at first and push students to use their knowledge of related names, dates, and places to arrive at a high-quality estimation of the target bit? This approach puts the onus on students to think critically and tie the pieces together. They can still go back and check their accuracy later, and might even have fun doing so. In the meantime, they have reinforced a broader, stronger, longer-lasting mental organization of those bits.

Finally, doing things the hard way can help students understand how the tools they typically use actually work. Tackling a few tricky translations themselves from a foreign language to English might help them see how the websites do it, and why they are not 100 percent dependable. Calculating a few interest rates from simple investment options themselves could help them recognize how various weighted factors contribute to the "bottom line" spit out by the software. Building some graphics from the ground up might help them determine which prepackaged ones would be most appropriate for a project or presentation in the future. By doing these things the hard way, students become more informed end users and consumers. They gain deeper insights into the subject matter by better understanding the tools they are using from the inside out. Furthermore, experiences like these could be the impetus for certain students to pursue important career work developing the next generation of tools in language translation, financial consulting, or graphic design.

Doing things the hard way in class is, well, not always easy! Teachers must see enough merit in doing so to be willing to take this high road once in a while. We have a responsibility to show students the best ways to do what the leaders in our respective fields do. Usually, those ways are the most current, efficient, and productive—for getting the job done. Not necessarily for getting the student educated. As you contemplate your approach to your next activity in class, think about the entire scope of benefits students will gain. Is there any room for tackling some aspect of that project the hard way? Will it bear benefits otherwise unavailable to them? Will it take too much time or energy to accomplish? Is it worth it, all things considered? Putting these questions into the larger perspective of the project will help you see how students can go both the easy and hard routes at different times to make the most of their experience in your class.

KEY IDEAS:

- Doing things the hard way on occasion can provide big benefits.
- We must balance practical factors and learning depth to decide when it is appropriate.

WAIT

It is one of the hardest things to do. It comes in two varieties: required and voluntary. We often wait because it is required, in line at the grocery store, online for a file to download, or anywhere for traffic to start moving again. To make this involuntary waiting bearable, we have to develop patience and learn to make the most of the downtime. The more powerful type of waiting is self-imposed. We decide purposefully to wait rather than making a move right now, and may be glad we did. Teaching offers more of these opportunities than the sands and stars combined, but here are just a few examples to get you thinking.

Any type of response in teaching involves timing, and therefore the opportunity to wait. During challenging interactions with students, phone calls or meetings with parents, or discussions with colleagues or administrators, waiting can make a big difference in the outcome.

I once had a new student with a pretty big attitude decide to insert a crass, inappropriate joke into our otherwise civilized conversation on the very first day of class. She was clearly "testing the room." The problem was that the joke wasn't actually funny; it just didn't quite work. Luckily, I happened to notice that no one in the room was laughing and decided to just wait a few moments. That thick, dark, humbling silence nipped the problem in the bud for the rest of the semester.

In classroom interactions, waiting can also help you look into the potential reasons for a confusion question to provide a quality response, or allow everyone in the room some time to ponder before you address it.

Another classroom situation ripe for waiting is when you are about to follow up on a concept in much more depth or present something new right now that should actually come later. Sometimes, it is certainly in students' best interest to take a detour in the moment and address something that has developed spontaneously, but at other times, it may provide cause for regret, as it pulls us too far off track. Perhaps the most challenging part of waiting under these circumstances is learning to curb our excitement at the moment we recognize a chance to make a connection, seeing that we can still make the connection later—as planned—with perhaps greater overall effect.

In addition to momentary decisions to wait, opportunities may arise for longer-term purposeful delay. We all know there are certain times we are best equipped, mentally and physically, to do certain things. Be proactive about aligning those activities with those times. For example, you might purposefully wait to ponder big decisions or do major planning until you are in a healthy, energized frame of mind. You might wait to write an e-mail to all parents until you have had time to clear your head, organize your thoughts, and check your motives. You might wait to make a schedule or curricular shift until you have had the time to check all the details carefully with colleagues.

The fast-paced day of typical teachers tends to breed snap decisions and quick action. Often, that is exactly what is needed, but sometimes a bit of waiting can save the day. Ponder those moments in your past where you decided to wait in the midst of a challenge, or perhaps did not even know about the challenge until after the fact, and it somehow worked itself out. If we are too hasty in our actions we can complicate the problems that arise, so be willing to create a bit of extra time for things to settle or even clarify themselves.

KEY IDEAS:

- Waiting is tough, but if done purposefully, it can improve our interactions significantly.
- Keep up the pace in your room, but pause and postpone when it will be more beneficial.

UNCOVER COURSE CONTENT ON
A NEED-TO-KNOW BASIS

What do school students really need to know? This is the question that guides the big-picture decision-making in curriculum development. Asking and answering this question generates national standards, student learning objectives, and large-scale assessments. It guides the process of periodic evaluation and revision of course curriculum to keep it current and effective.

Equally important, though, are smaller, more frequent decisions about what students need to know at the classroom level on a daily basis. These choices show up fast and furious, one after another, challenging teachers to determine quickly and decisively whether a theme, idea, or topic is truly something necessary or just an interesting extra that could be saved for later or bypassed altogether.

What sorts of "extras" pop into your mind as you teach? Are there things that *you* currently find interesting but that probably will not engage students? For example, you may see an obvious parallel between your fifth-graders' understanding of percentages and your current deliberations about your retirement plan but maybe you are all alone in your excitement. Things that are appropriate for much more advanced students in your field? Perhaps you can explain convincingly the relationship between the funny poem your fourth graders just read and the finer points of the history of iambic pentameter, but they are not quite ready for that. Things that might demonstrate your high command of the material but take you too far off topic? As you walk your high schoolers through constitutional law, you might feel the urge to invoke your prior career as a high-profile attorney, but it is just not the right time. Things that may satisfy a single student's curiosity but leave the rest of the class in a fog? Providing additional explanations about Mandarin grammar to an eager standout student is enticing, but not everyone is prepared to understand it.

Clearly, decisions regarding need-to-know information depend on the intersection of people and time. In its original use for security operations, "need-to-know information" is made available only to those who have a direct reason to use it and the accompanying clearance. *At a given time.* In other words, at any given point in time only some people need to have that information, or for any given people only at some point in time will they need it. Some knowledge that was previously not "need-to-know" might become so when a person is promoted or reassigned to a different position. Decision-makers must decide early on which intersections of people and time will require the sharing of that knowledge.

Similarly, in education we need to view our students carefully *in time* to determine who needs to know what. We need to have a perspective on their history, a vision for their future, and a clear picture of what they need to function fully in our environment right now. An occasional bonus bit of knowledge or extra illustration can be inspiring, sure, but stretching too far from what is essential on a regular basis can cause a lot of headaches. Keep it manageable. Keep it reasonable. Give students plenty of what they need to know and leave the rest for another day.

KEY IDEAS:

- Consistently determining what students need to know helps us focus their learning.
- Timing is an essential factor in making these decisions and keeping learning flowing.

ASK *REAL* QUESTIONS AS OFTEN
AS POSSIBLE IN CLASS

Questions. We love 'em, don't we? We use them for so many wonderful reasons in class, truly a primary tool in our pedagogy kit. Questions prompt answers, and manipulating various aspects of those questions can influence learning direction and pace in beautiful, powerful ways. What we ask students and how we ask it can make all the light bulbs go on. And stay on.

Not all questions beg the same sorts of answers though. Teachers might use any of the following types on a daily basis:

• Review questions that help students practice or repeat correct answers;
• Leading questions, in which the answer is pre-planned, targeted, and expected;
• Loaded questions that carry some inherent assumption; and
• Pressing questions that push students to carry their thinking further.

All of these can serve their intended purpose well, but it may be worth our while to examine the intended purpose of each and the balance in which we use them.

Review questions help students reinforce information they have already assimilated. We might employ these prior to an assessment or before moving on to the next unit. They could be spoken or written down, directed to one individual or "up for grabs," formal or informal. They might be included in a game or competition, all for the purpose of getting students to rehearse the material in their minds and maintain it more clearly and fully. The question-answer interaction is appealing for review tasks because students have to generate a thought themselves, even if it might be triggered by the content of the question.

Leading questions are similar to review questions, but can be used for information that is not yet known by, or not yet clear to, students. We use leading questions when we shroud an answer we want in the form of an essentially fake question. The classic examples are from the courtroom: "Would that not lead us to believe that Mr. So-and-So was in the right place, at the right time, with a good reason to commit this crime?" Our leading questions in the classroom might not be so bold and aggressive, but they can be just as insincere and perhaps unfair. "Should we always wear safety goggles to protect our eyes when working with dangerous chemicals?" "Do we need to find the length of the other two sides of the right triangle before we find the perimeter of the rectangle that includes it?" and "Are these rhythms the same ones we saw in the first measures of the song?" Just like a great lawyer, we have done the thinking for our students prior to the exchange; all they have to do is follow us into the welcoming trap. Leading questions are efficient, but students might not learn much from the experience. They also might subconsciously start to doubt the quality of our questions for future reference.

Loaded questions carry some bias or assumption that muddies the waters of classroom exchanges. Teachers often use them, wittingly or unwittingly, to make a point or float an opinion, cleverly masked as a conceptual question. Again, the concept comes from the courtroom: "Ms. So-and-So, what produces this urge within you to steal [when trying to convict the defendant of robbery]?" The prosecutor is nesting an attacking assumption within a question that sounds more broad and genuine. In the classroom, it may show up less personally and more subtly. "Why, then, is democracy the best form of government?" "During what time period did Country X invade [or 'liberate' or 'attack'] the people of Countries Y and Z?" The first, and biggest, challenge with loaded questions may be simply realizing we are doing it. Any of the three verbs in the last example could be loading the question. We have to investigate our own assumptions to make sure they don't creep into otherwise well-intended questions.

Pressing questions are helpful for pushing students' thinking to the next level. The students all know the basic information cold, so the time has come to dig deeper. The teacher still knows "the" answers to these questions, or at least the gist of them, but is pressing students to take the next cognitive step on their own. The ball is in the students' court, usually inspiring higher-level thinking than review or leading questions can accomplish. "How?" and "Why?" can be good starters for pressing questions, as they nudge students to go beyond the surface and apply their higher-order thinking skills. Pressing questions actually *sound* a lot more genuine right away when asked: "Well, then, why do you suppose it works that way?" Teachers' vocal inflection signifies an important prompt on the horizon that might actually require some thought, not just simple recall or clue awareness. And still, the answers are known and expected.

Given all of the above, and other types of questions you may use, let us consider one more: *real* questions, questions for which you do not know the answer, questions that you may have thought of before, but have not had a chance to think *about* enough just yet, questions that might arise in your mind spontaneously during class that you are not sure how you would answer, and questions that, if you asked genuinely in front of your students, might even make you, the alleged "know-it-all" in the room, feel vulnerable.

Most readers would probably readily agree that students learn a lot from us by what we do. How we think, and how we express not only our thoughts but also our *thinking*, can be extremely beneficial to students. Asking genuine questions, to which you really do not know the answer, is probably the best and perhaps only way for students to learn to do likewise. You probably cannot afford to make all of your questions real questions, for the sake of pacing and engagement, but a real question from time to time can make learning so much deeper and lasting. Take a chance.

KEY IDEAS:

- Teachers can employ several types of questions in class for specific learning purposes.
- Asking *real* questions, without pre-planned answers, can boost students' thinking skills.

Chapter 4

You

IN THE CLASSROOM, GET YOURSELF OUT OF THE PICTURE EARLY AND OFTEN

If our main goal is for students to grow as much as possible in every way, we should do our best to keep their path free of unnecessary obstructions. Obstruction #1 on the list at any given time might just be you. What a fascinating line of work—determining what students need from us and offering it to them in creative ways, all while stepping aside at just the right moments to allow them to go it alone for their long-term benefit.

As they learn to learn, students need opportunities to trust themselves, try things alone, and build confidence. They not only need to be comfortable asking for help and seeking answers from others but also to struggle by themselves for their own good. By providing them with a mixture of these experiences, students begin to realize how all of it contributes to their learning. And so do you. To help students get the most out of their time with you, ironically, you have to plan for them to grow independently of you. Consider getting out of the picture early and often.

Let's look at each of the two descriptors, "early" and "often." "Early" might refer to "early in the marking period," "early in the class meeting," or "early in the five-minute activity." No matter the length of time allotted, getting out of the picture early means sending your students off on their own as soon as it is feasible. This may ultimately entail a series of cycles between teacher prompts and student activity. The idea is to provide only minimal front matter on your part so that students get truly engaged as soon as possible, through *actions* requiring their learning energy. In so doing, they get locked in to the learning process quickly and discover that their tangible contributions will be required in your room.

127

If you provide minimal front matter to get students off to a quick start, you will likely need to reenter relatively soon to keep things moving. The same question applies with each interjection: How little can you introduce while still providing enough to keep them going? The less you provide, the more they have to generate. So, as soon as they are adequately prepared to contribute again, get out of the way.

Obviously, we can take this too far. Too little instruction is no good. However, too much instruction is no good either. Scout out moments in which you can disappear, moments when students can carry on swiftly and naturally as they manage that next leap themselves. Get in the habit of stepping aside just as they reach that point, not too soon and not too late. The key is to play your role in this classroom story masterfully, delivering your lines at just the right moment and supporting the protagonists in perhaps unnoticed but indispensable ways.

KEY IDEAS:

- Students need us to get them started, but they also need us to give them space.
- Balancing our contributions with theirs can be a constant series of fruitful cycles.

BETTER TO GIVE IN AND LEARN SOMETHING THAN TO INSIST YOU KNOW IT ALL

Professional teaching assumes expertise. Students, parents, administrators, colleagues, and the wider community expect that we know our material inside and out, that we have experience applying it appropriately, and that we can skillfully guide others through it. Being labeled an expert brings great responsibility that we should take seriously. Even for the humblest of teachers, instilling confidence in your students that you know what you are doing and are capable of helping them is tantamount to a successful class. After all, who wants to follow leaders who are unsure or unequipped themselves?

On the other hand, who wants to follow leaders who are so focused on being experts that they forget how to learn something new? An open, inquisitive mind is essential for encouraging open, inquisitive minds. When a surprise comes your way in class, especially related specifically to your field of expertise, it is better to give in and learn something than to insist you know it all.

The truth is that you probably don't know it all. Even in your particular area of academic interest. Nobody does. Many, including you, may know an awful lot, much more perhaps than the average citizen, but each of us is prone to encounter new ideas, information, tools, and trends along the way. Sometimes, those enlightening bits come right from students.

Several reasons beckon us to let down our shield of expertise and soak up knowledge like a novice, right there in front of our students. It adds to our expertise, making us that much more effective in future teaching. It keeps the educational environment open, truly and tangibly honoring the input and serving as a model for future classroom interactions. It supports proactive learning, putting students in productive rather than receptive pedagogical positions. Finally, it gives students an opportunity to *watch us learn*. Savor that opportunity because it may be the most important thing you show them.

Some time ago, I taught piano lessons to a high school English teacher. At our first meeting, I asked him what had caused him in his mid-thirties to take up lessons as a beginner. He gave a couple of answers I had heard from adults before: "I have always wanted to play music." "I never had the chance as a kid." "I hear that it is good for mental and physical health." However, he finished with a reason I will never forget: "I also just want my 9-year-old daughter to see me struggling to learn something new and difficult." He explained that sometimes she expressed that her parents seemed to know everything and that she knew very little. She felt overwhelmed by the work it would take to master anything, and often gave up too soon. The father's teaching and parenting instincts wanted to help her with that process. He realized that the best way

was to genuinely tackle something large and difficult himself, giving her better
perspective and opening himself to vulnerable moments of observation—a bril-
liant move on his part that made a huge difference.

This father was far from being an expert in music and his teaching wisdom
helped him see how that could ultimately benefit his daughter. In a related
way, even though we may have quite a bit of expertise in our subject area,
we still have room to grow. Doing so in plain view can be the best thing that
ever happens to our students—and us. If you were to sketch a diagram of your
relationship to your students, would it look like two different entities facing
each other with one spewing forth and the other soaking up? Or, might it look
like two similar entities moving along the same path, one a certain distance
ahead and leading by example?

KEY IDEAS:

- We all have plenty still to discover even about our primary area of
  expertise.
- Be willing to get on the learning path, stay on it, and take your students
  with you.

THOUGHTS ARE A DIME A DOZEN; QUALITY THOUGHTS ARE PRECIOUS AND FEW

In fact, thoughts are much cheaper than a dime a dozen. Thoughts come to us quite freely, at times so quickly and constantly that we may not even be aware of them. We are simply engulfed. A normal day of teaching gives us a great deal to think about: students, concepts, materials, schedule, communications, meetings, logistics, grading, and more planning. Our minds may feel absolutely stuffed with thoughts, a large majority of which are superfluous, irrelevant, or even downright counterproductive. We have to find ways to quickly discard those, or even cancel them preemptively, to focus our attention on the quality thoughts that really deserve our time and energy.

Accomplishing this begins with some sort of thought observation. We begin to notice our thoughts from a bit of distance, to see how and when they appear, what patterns they take, how one thought leads to another, and why. We begin to recognize characteristics of "quality" thoughts, according to our own unique definition, helping us make the most of this formidable tool called the human mind. We begin to observe how thoughts lead to words and actions, and subsequently leverage our awareness of quality thoughts to make every move count in the classroom. Or at least try our best.

Thinking, of course, is one of the most personal, individual things we do. It is difficult to "compare notes" about thinking or to help each other with problems or challenges at the thought level. Even when we can describe our thoughts and thought patterns to each other, we are discussing something that depends on individual experiences, projections, needs, and desires. However, a deeper look into our own thoughts beckons, and all of us could probably benefit from probing the balance between useful and useless ones.

As we observe our thoughts, each of us has to decide for ourselves which are deserving of the discard pile; here are a few categories to consider:

- repetitive assumptions about a student's prior behavior;
- anxious thoughts about the outcome of a class or activity;
- irrelevant ideas that distract from your attention in the moment;
- regrets about forgetting something or making a mistake;
- concerns about your image in students' or colleagues' eyes;
- judgments of students that do not contribute directly to their learning; and
- self-reminders about how busy or tired you are.

None of these is necessarily useless to all teachers, but any or all of them may be useless to some. Ponder additional categories of dispensable thoughts and target them for gradual (or perhaps sudden) removal. Following through on this will give those precious and few quality thoughts a more direct path to your full attention. Finding the needle in the haystack becomes easier as you toss aside larger and larger chunks of the pile, putting aside what is unnecessary and focusing on what is worthwhile.

KEY IDEAS:

- Teachers entertain myriad thoughts throughout the day, some helpful and some not.
- Explore your thoughts and thought patterns, gradually discarding what is not conducive.

ASK YOURSELF "WHY?" AND "WHY NOT?" FREQUENTLY

Perhaps the most famous, and dreadfully poor, reason for doing something is "Well, because we've always done it that way." It is so famous, in fact, that people state it sarcastically and playfully in institutional discussions. Yet, this response rears its ugly head, directly or indirectly, in way too many self-evaluations. We are asking the right question but failing with our answer. Brainstorming in response to the question "Why are we doing this?" should either produce better reasons or cause some change in the practice. The only way either will happen is if we continue to ask the question with a genuine spirit of investigation.

The good news is that the simplest form of self-evaluative "Why?" questioning occurs within a single person. You as a teacher can ask yourself "Why?" frequently in the privacy of your own mind. You can ponder the possible reasons efficiently and honestly, discovering what may be lurking behind a particular classroom philosophy, concept, or activity. You have relatively high autonomy over the self-evaluation process and your options for future change. The bad news is that we probably do not actually ask the question frequently or earnestly enough.

As we explore why our class is as it is, are we willing to question our own assumptions about students and curriculum, our school culture, the experts in our field, the textbook, the standards, our curriculum, our colleagues, and our mentors? Do we have not only the courage to question them but also the willingness to commit the time and energy it takes to probe what is behind our decisions that ultimately affect students?

Start with questions closest to home, involving just you and your students—that is, questions you can actually answer or solve:

- Why am I covering this topic so thoroughly (or so cursorily)?
- Why am I introducing this concept before that one?
- Why do I allow students so much (or little) time for this project?
- Why do I set up the room this way?
- Why do I (or don't I) insist that students raise their hands to answer or ask?
- Why do I grade attendance the way I do? Why do I grade attendance at all?
- Why do the students, and I, seem to get tired right around 1:15 every day?
- Why do I always begin class by speaking?
- Why do I feel slightly uneasy in situation x, y, or z?

These are just a smattering of the sorts of questions you might ask yourself, but notice that they cover a broad range of factors in your room. "Why?" is a highly versatile question, begging an honest, solid rationale, or a meaningful shift from the status quo.

The obvious counterpart to "Why?" questions is "Why not?" questions. Sometimes, these can be paired as a follow-up to a "Why?" question that currently yields a weak reason. For example, "Why do I set up the room the way it is? . . . Because that is the way my mentor always did it" . . . then, "Why not move the chairs into smaller clusters with my desk against the adjacent wall?" Other "Why not?" questions stand alone, arriving more spontaneously:

- Why not push students a bit, or a lot, harder on this project?
- Why not start class right on time from now on, whether students are ready or not?
- Why not smile more often when it's genuine and appropriate?
- Why not institute a self-reporting system for completion of additional practice?
- Why not invite more guest speakers to class?
- Why not designate student leaders on a rotating basis more frequently?
- Why not take students further outside the classroom more often?
- Why not do this next project right along with them and let them see me struggle?
- Why not delay this unit in the curricular sequence?

Some of these "Why not?" questions may be rhetorical, which is a fancy way of stating that you have already decided to do something. Others, however, may require some serious thought. Maybe there are great reasons why not to institute a self-reporting system or delay a unit. Either way, you have given the options fair consideration, creating potential for change and improvement.

Generally speaking, "Why?" questions as described here scrutinize what already is, while "Why not?" questions evaluate what could be. Putting these two tools into regular practice can reveal a lot about what is driving your classroom. Be willing to ask, and answer, these questions frequently and honestly. You are certainly the best person for the job.

KEY IDEAS:

- Regularly questioning our own reasons for what we do is a healthy practice.
- Asking yourself "Why not?" frequently can transform student learning dramatically.

ACCEPT ALL ADVICE GRACIOUSLY; THEN PICK
AND CHOOSE WISELY

As teachers, plenty of advice comes our way—excellent, awful, and everything in between. Some is solicited, some not. Some is relevant, some not. Advice may come from anyone—colleagues, administrators, parents, students, or members of your school's surrounding community. It may arrive face-to-face, by phone, by letter, by text, or e-mail. You may receive it directly from the source or by word of mouth "through the grapevine." In all cases, consider accepting that advice graciously. You can determine its usefulness later.

Perhaps the main reason to accept all advice with open arms initially is that it will encourage more advice. If members of your educational community learn to identify you as someone who is close-minded, who thinks he already has the answers, and who prefers not to listen to others' perspectives, they will be reluctant to offer you their opinions in the future. If they know you to be someone who readily and thoroughly hears and absorbs their ideas, they will be willing to share more. Even if you ultimately do not act in alignment with a given suggestion they know that you heard them well, and perhaps they will strive to offer an even better idea next time around!

The challenge with accepting advice as a teacher is that we have such limited time and flexibility to put things into action—and so much advice to field. This should prompt your development of a very important skill—determining quickly and definitively which advice will ultimately be helpful to your students. Does the administrator's suggestion bear the students' best interests in mind or would it just make the school look better that day? Does the parent's proposal benefit your whole class or really just his child? Does your colleague's recommendation really apply to your social studies classes or just to her language arts classes? Are your students' requests well conceived or short-sighted? You may even recognize the answer to these questions in the moment of hearing them, but you still have the option to accept the advice with a bit of sincere gratitude. The key word here is "sincere," because you must be honestly glad these people offered you their input even when you suspect it will not work this time. Humans sniff out fake gratitude exceptionally well.

A useful way to look at how well we receive advice is to consider how we give it. When do you offer suggestions to others? How do you offer them? What triggers those contributions? What are the intentions behind your advice? What do you hope it will accomplish? How do you expect the receiver to respond, in that moment and down the road? Would that response affect your decision about whether or how to offer more advice in the future?

Most people give and receive advice regularly in some sort of balance, so paying attention to how it functions from both sides of the table can be helpful.

We often think of advice as something given by a wiser, more experienced person to a rookie.

I remember distinctly a question from a student in my capstone teacher preparation course: "I'm a little nervous about older teachers looking down on me and treating me like a newbie when I get my first job; did that ever happen to you?" I replied with an unmistakably sarcastic, "No, no, that NEVER happened to me!" Lots of laughs, but I went on to assure them quite seriously that young teachers have much to offer our educational system. I encouraged them that even in the toughest veteran-rookie relationships, they must be prepared to offer what they can, and that age and experience do not necessarily produce the best ideas every time.

Just as the students became visibly content and empowered by this perspective, I dropped the other shoe with a pretty loud bang: "And that also means that people younger and less experienced than you—for example, your students— will have better ideas than yours sometimes." Eyes darted back and forth as these pre-service teachers questioned the common belief that undergraduate training somehow magically transforms people from students who know next-to- nothing into teachers who have it all figured out. They had prepared themselves to receive lots of advice from older colleagues, and were hoping to be able to offer it in return, but to field excellent advice or stellar ideas from students? That would be quite a feat.

The fact that good advice can come in such a diversity of packages is a beautiful testament to the collective effort required for quality education. Veteran, first-year, and pre-service teachers may all be reading this; hopefully, it offers some perspective for all three. As we grow older and more experienced in our profession, we can all too easily begin to think we know it all. It comes naturally because if we are doing things right we certainly know better than before, but knowing better than before is not knowing all. More experienced teachers should offer any help they can to newer colleagues, but should also listen carefully for good ideas coming their way. Remaining open to the suggestions of others, even those not expected to have the most valuable insights, is an important way to keep growing and helping our students. For early-career teachers and those just now preparing to start, be willing to offer your input even when it seems not to be regarded very highly or is even openly rejected. You never know when your idea may catch on.

Finally, for all of us: Accept all advice graciously; then pick and choose wisely. This is what keeps education moving in the right direction, providing better and better learning opportunities for our students based on the collective understanding and experience of the greatest number of caring stakeholders. None of us has to go it alone; take along as many helpful collaborators as you wish in the form of their shared perspectives and fine ideas. How's that for good advice?

KEY IDEAS:

- Advice arrives quickly and plentifully at work; teachers must evaluate it efficiently.
- Accepting all advice sincerely generally encourages more of it; be choosy later.

TAKE YOUR OWN ADVICE

Getting and giving advice is a daily balance for teachers, with the potential to generate substantial positive change in our schools. We learn to accept and offer advice efficiently and graciously, to quickly and wisely determine which bits truly would benefit our students, and even to identify consistently helpful and unhelpful sources of advice for future interactions and decisions. We hope that others really believe in the advice they give us; that is, that they are thoroughly convinced that it is the best route for us to take. We certainly should be able to assume that the advice we give others carries the same fine intentions and thoughtful deliberation. Often overlooked, ironically, is the cream of the crop: taking our own advice.

When we offer a suggestion to colleagues or students with their best interests truly in mind, we already know the honesty and purity of our words. We also maintain those recommendations very clearly in our memory because they came from within, not from external sources. The icing on the cake is checking all facets of our own teaching to make sure that we are applying that same advice to our daily work.

A similar theme arises famously in families. A parent or grandparent tells a child not to do something, truly for her own good, but then does essentially the same thing in a different scenario or on a different level. Parents may be told that their children behave a certain way because that is how they themselves behave, but perhaps it is hard to recognize at first. The parents are either willfully maintaining a double standard or, more likely, not seeing the opportunity to take their own advice.

A clear parallel can be found with teachers and students. You are probably aware already of the effects of certain teachers' personalities and actions on students' behavior. The same group of students, for instance, may act quite differently with one teacher than with another. Clearly, the teachers are contributing at least some, if not most, of the difference in outcomes. Something is "rubbing off" on students, for better or for worse.

Teachers who find themselves perpetually disappointed by students' relative level of functioning in their room should take a close look at what they themselves are communicating regularly. Investigating this input in light of the advice they give to others provides a powerful tool. Both the problem and the solution can be found within. The advice has already been prepared for external sharing, and perhaps shared many times; now, it needs to be matched with an internal challenge to solve the problem at hand.

For example, a teacher may frequently say, in so many ways, that being on time is really important. The advice may take the form of direct verbalization to students arriving late to class or purposefully anxious glances at the clock as colleagues arrive late to a meeting. Yet the teacher always finds herself rushing out the door at the last minute in the morning because she simply "cannot" get up quite early enough. She always slips into the back door of the school at the last minute before homeroom and even if nobody notices it, her advice to others somehow loses its power. She does not truly own it yet because she has not put it into practice for herself.

In another scenario, a teacher is known for his pet phrase "Never say 'I can't' in my classroom." He seems to value self-empowerment and positive, proactive thinking above all else for his students, but actually does not take his own advice on a regular basis. He finds himself putting things off, asking others to take on tasks he sees as highly challenging, and engaging in self-defeating self-talk frequently. He seems to be speaking to others the advice he needs to take himself.

As the old saying goes, "We teach what we are learning." Perhaps looking at these two examples in light of this perspective can reduce the severity of the situation. We need not lament the fact that we are not currently taking our own advice, or regret that we missed opportunities to do so in the past. Just reverse the famous phrase and be sure to learn what you are teaching. Practice what you preach. Take your own advice.

The teacher who barely makes it to school on time could set the alarm ten minutes earlier every day, exactly the amount of time she needs to be able to drive like a normal person and stroll through the main entrance calmly and comfortably. The "never say can't" teacher could pick a small task right now that is holding a bit of "you can't" power over him and decide to give it a shot, no matter what, with a commitment to full patience, hard work, and no fear of failure.

When we take our own advice, we capitalize on the fact that the problem-solution cycle takes place completely inside ourselves. We find that problems are fixed efficiently and permanently because the solution already resides within us and is much more likely to remain there over the long term. We also generate profound power when offering that advice to others in the future because we have taken ownership of it ourselves through lived experience, making it truly ours to give.

KEY IDEAS:

- Your best advice may be dwelling right inside you already.
- Pay attention to the suggestions you offer others and be sure you use them yourself.

SET ASIDE TIME PERIODICALLY FOR YOUR MIND
TO CATCH UP WITH ITSELF

The fifth-grade science teacher walks into class with the latest headlines absolutely *buzzing* in his head: the updated weather forecast for the weekend, news from the political race, and changes in a state law that may affect his health insurance. He had trouble sleeping last night because of some other news he caught on social media just before bed, and this morning instead of thinking those issues all the way through on his commute he listened to more talk radio. As he starts the first activity with students, his mind is everywhere except where it should be.

The seventh-grade computer applications teacher arrives to school suddenly remembering that she forgot to slow down and resolve a number of questions that lingered after yesterday's very challenging class. A student had commented that one of the concepts probed on the unit test last week did not seem correct. It sparked several questions in her mind about the content in the unit and she had resolved to think it all through, clarify the problem areas, and perhaps create an opportunity to remedy the faulty test if needed. After dinner last night, though, she found a fascinating documentary on the latest technological advances in robotics and simply could not turn it off. As she drifted off to sleep, her brain continued to spin on robots and when she awoke in the morning the planned contemplation slipped her mind until the bell rang. Now there was no time to do that precious thinking.

These examples offer a glimpse into how teachers can absorb information that may be relevant and important and decide to dedicate needed time to it, only to then inadvertently absorb still more information instead of finishing the mental work at hand. The mind has not had a chance to fully process something that is already calling for its attention before it picks up something new that will require still more of the same. It needs a chance to catch up with itself.

The mind is constantly seeking new material. It is curious and wants to be fed. If we don't give our minds the time and space to process things fully, however, the feeding will be a bit like mealtime for a toddler—a big mess with half the food on the floor. We have to pace our information intake and subsequent pondering in tandem so that we truly make the most of what we absorb every day. This may require a proactive decision to set aside some time periodically to complete the cycle.

"Periodically" depends on the scope of the material and the time available. For instance, you might set aside every Friday's prep period as a chance to reflect on the week's class meetings and tie up any loose ends. More short-term, you might commit to five minutes of quiet time every morning to gather your thoughts before the school day starts. More long-term, you might dedicate a few days of winter or summer break to a mental retreat, checking in on the "big picture" of your teaching, resolving any internal questions and concerns, and taking care of other unfinished cognitive business.

The two teachers in our examples likely would have benefited from purposefully putting a temporary stop to any new information and allowing their minds to finish what was already started. This decision could yield at least two levels of positive results. They would be more likely to meet students fresh, in the moment, with a clear head and quality ideas, and they would be more likely to help students learn to do the same. Students have an amazing sense about the quality of mindset the teacher brings to class each day. We have regular opportunities to show them a mind that is caught up with itself and ready to help others.

KEY IDEAS:

- A cluttered mind leaves little room for clear thinking.
- Gathering new information may not be as helpful as sorting out what you already have.

A SINGLE INTERNAL CHANGE CAN BE GREATER
THAN MANY EXTERNAL ONES

People often overlook a simple but profound truth, that everything—
everything—in your world is processed through you. The tallest structures,
most significant events, most powerful people, and most amazing experiences
all happen through you. Philosophers can debate whether an objective world
continues on without your presence; that is not the point here. The point is
that *for you* all the stuff of everyday life has to be perceived and evaluated
internally, subsequently producing your response back out to the world.

The real power of this recognition lies in your ability to observe even the
subtlest movements within yourself. Your observations, thoughts, feelings,
reactions, and memories are yours, practically impossible to communicate
adequately to anyone else. Yet, you know them well and can come to know
them even better. Keen awareness of internal events can make dramatic
changes in how you view your external environment and operate within it.

When teaching, we field lots of external events in short order. We may
be monitoring students' verbal and nonverbal communication, noticing off-
task behavior, hearing surprise distractions from the intercom, and checking
the clock. It can feel like a tornado of activity, all happening at once, and
all while delivering a steady stream of sequential concepts and interesting
prompts. All of the external stimuli are only really happening to us through
our internal processing, though, so their importance and meaning depend on
how we field them.

We know that two people can describe their experience of the same event
in two very different ways. The internal approach each of them takes to the
event colors what they actually perceive, attend to, realize, and remember.
They are intrigued by different parts of what they experience and may produce highly contrasting reactions as a result. What they took into it affects
what they take away from it.

At school we have infinite opportunities to notice and adapt what is happening inside us as we perceive what is happening outside us, and a single
internal change can be greater than many external ones. We teachers tend to
watch carefully what is happening around us in our rooms and schools and
seek to change those external circumstances to improve them. Great! We
also need to remind ourselves that all of that work is happening by way of
our internal selves. If we notice something unwanted popping up externally
again and again or see something missing out there that would be beneficial,
perhaps we need to look inward for the best solution too.

This inward looking is difficult to describe because our levels of understanding of ourselves may be widely different from others'. However, a few

general examples might spark your own recognition of more specific and personally pertinent ones. For example,

- Can you adjust, faster or slower, your internal reaction time to a question or comment?
- Can you catch confirmation welling up inside you early enough to avoid giving away to the whole class that an answer was correct?
- Can you notice internal reactions of disappointment, pride, contention, or excitement quickly enough to determine consciously the best way to express them?
- Can you discover your subtlest thoughts and feelings about planning, preparation, and reflection to allow these processes to function fully and freely for your students' benefit?

Naturally, this level of introspection can be problematic if we overanalyze what is taking place. We have to keep the pace going in class and attend fully to what is happening in front of us. However, even an occasional, single dive down deeper can have lasting effects. Noticing something happening within us, recognizing how it affects everything else, and determining how to change it to make it more effective is a far-reaching shift, because it improves not only the situation at hand but alters how we show up in subsequent circumstances. Just like two people experiencing the same situation differently, the internal processing you currently bring and that which you could be bringing can produce striking contrasts in responses and results. You are the only one that can tackle this project—a unique responsibility and a wonderful freedom.

KEY IDEAS:

- Our internal functioning affects every bit of our external interactions.
- We can create broad, powerful changes in our environment through a bit of inner work.

WHEN WORDS AND ACTIONS FALL SHORT, INVESTIGATE THE THOUGHTS THAT PRODUCED THEM

In my undergraduate education courses, students peer-teach in class to sharpen their skills. An essential part of the process is using a video recording of their lessons to observe and assess their own teaching afterward. I press students in their self-evaluations to note detailed occurrences of subtle things they would like to investigate. In my capstone course for upper-level undergraduates, the students manage to capture very small but powerful moves, perhaps even a single word or momentary action that either helped or hindered the day's progress in a substantial way. This may seem like the furthest one could carry the exercise, but one crucial extension remains, one that only the individual can explore: the thoughts that preceded that teacher move.

It is perhaps the most elusive, pervasive, subtle, and certainly powerful part of the equation. What was happening inside you just as you made that verbal response, facial expression, gesture, or physical shift? What thought or succession of thoughts led you to speak the instructions in a slightly different order than planned or to use voice inflection to color your words a certain way? What were you thinking as you reacted to student confusion and made a game-changing decision regarding small group assignments?

We can see and hear others' words and actions, either live or on recordings, very clearly. We know fairly confidently what we witness and we can even discuss it with others. Only each of us by ourselves, though, can explore our own thoughts clearly and honestly as they relate to our resultant words and actions. We should do so as frequently and deeply as possible. Taking this additional step does not need to be prompted or required by an outside source; simply get in the habit of noticing how your thinking guides what you produce moment by moment. This is helpful both to highlight what is working well and to nip troubles in the bud.

A great way to explore this relationship is through routine events in your life. We take many of our thoughts for granted, so paying closer attention to them can be surprisingly interesting. Look back with 20/20 hindsight to consider what string of thoughts ultimately caused you to choose what you had for lunch today, or what information, calculations, and conclusions took you to the hardware store before the supermarket on your way home from school. You may find that quite a few thoughts lined up and fed each other systematically to make that final, relatively unimportant result happen. By shining light on the relationship between thoughts and actions you begin to develop more specific awareness of your thinking and prepare yourself for situations in which it may have more crucial consequences.

Many days, we teachers feel like we lack the time even to look back at the obvious stuff, the observable moves we made in the classroom across a systematic sequence of interactions with students. Try to find time to review those moments, especially the salient ones, whenever possible. When you do, though, look a bit further than what happened externally to uncover what happened internally too. You can learn a lot about yourself that way—valuable things for the next time around.

KEY IDEAS:

- Each of us has a truly unique opportunity to explore our thoughts and what they produce.
- Observe the relationship between your thoughts and decisions in routine activities today.

ALL YOU CAN REALLY OFFER IS YOUR BEST SELF; OFFER IT ALWAYS

Teachers may encounter many tempting influences regarding how we should approach our craft. The latest video series, curriculum supplement, or online training seminar promises to make our classroom such a better place. Everyone from colleagues to students to parents to mentors is offering us advice and well-intentioned guidance. Amid all the external input vying for our attention we may be persuaded to think that "our teaching" is something separate from ourselves, that it is actually a thing we are trying to polish and perfect from a distance.

External resources and guidance can indeed help us keep our minds and options wide open. They may offer us new and valuable ideas that had never crossed our mind. However, every day what we really give our students, in a unique way, is ourselves. Perhaps the best thing we can offer them all the time, then, is our best self.

What might your "best self" mean? Every teacher's discoveries will likely be different, but a few pointers might get us started. Our best selves would certainly be highly conducive to student growth, very rarely or never standing in the way of progress due to personal conflicts, stubbornness, or shortsightedness. Our best selves would probably always be ready to help—truly help—in whatever ways our expert observations deem most appropriate. Our best selves would likely always speak and act how we would hope to see our students speak and act. Our best selves might be zealous learners, enthusiastic participants, and highly open to students' ideas.

"Sure," you say. "Aren't we always putting forth our best selves in the classroom?" That is the question. If even once in the past long while you have carried yourself in a way that you know was not your best, dig in there and discover what happened. What or who pushed your buttons? Why did you take the low road? How did circumstances seem to develop to the point where you made a decision that surprised even you and set back the class a bit? Did you let something influence you that you should have ignored? Or perhaps *not* listen to something that you should have heeded? Did you go against your better judgment or mistrust your gut? Did you create a double standard or an unfair ruling in the room?

None of these things is necessarily a huge problem, but exploring any and all of them can help us see how to offer students our best self even more consistently. Each of us develops uniquely as a teacher and all of us probably recognize opportunities to improve what we do at school in small but profound ways. Keep seeking and making those improvements. As you do, recognize that you cannot offer anything better than your best. Offer it always.

KEY IDEAS:

- Each of us can best monitor our own actions to be sure we are offering our best selves.
- Our moments of less-than-best efforts can go unnoticed; notice them and weed them out.

TO DO YOUR BEST TEACHING, BE SURE TO START
BY NEEDING NOTHING YOURSELF

At first, this suggestion may seem to apply only to brand new teachers or pre-service education majors. However, consider that "start" could refer to starting your career, starting a new school year, starting a new course after many years of teaching, or starting a new job at a different school in your district or far away. In all cases, when we prepare ourselves to teach students in some new situation, we must clear out our own needs first to be able to attend fully to theirs.

What might be some of our needs as teachers? Classroom resources, planning time, physical and mental energy, new skills, critical information, answers to lingering questions, satisfaction of curiosities, acknowledgment or praise by our administration, or admiration of our colleagues and students, to name a few. Most of the former items on the list can be resolved externally; some of the latter need to be resolved internally.

Have you cleared up all your own obstacles in anticipation of helping students clear theirs? The airlines' flight safety speeches provide a classic example of how this works [paraphrase]: "In the event of a loss of cabin pressure, put your own oxygen mask on before helping others." This may sound a bit selfish to someone hearing it for the first time, but the fact is that you cannot help someone else if you have lost consciousness. You must take care of yourself to be able to take care of others. Period. Needing something as a teacher can be much subtler than needing oxygen as a passenger. We may have to do some introspection to discover whether we are harboring some lack or gap that will not allow us to devote ourselves entirely to students when they need us most.

In the airplane analogy, we all truly *need* oxygen. There is no way to resolve the issue except through getting some from one of the masks. In teaching, however, part of our work in identifying and solving our own needs involves determining into which of two categories our needs actually fall. Some needs, like time for planning, can be resolved only by finding or creating some. The need has to be satisfied for it to go away. Other needs, like acknowledgment or praise from administrators, can be resolved by *letting go of the need* rather than attempting to fill it. In fact, knowing some administrators, that may be the only way to go!

Take a bit of introspection time to identify any needs you may have as a teacher, both obvious and subtle. Sort through them to determine which require specific, tangible solutions and which may be simply expendable, not really "needs" after all. If you feel that you can truly let those go, cross them off your list. Then, take the time to solve the ones that must be solved. When you can walk into the classroom without any needs yourself, you are prepared to offer students *all* of you. Nothing is more conducive to their success.

KEY IDEAS:

- Teachers may have obvious or subtle needs that can draw our energy away from students.
- Explore your own distinction between needs you must solve and "needs" you can drop.

IF YOU ARE STRESSED OUT ABOUT TEACHING, YOU MIGHT BE IN IT FOR THE WRONG REASONS

Let's be clear right away about the difference between "stressed out" and, say, "challenged." Teaching is no doubt a highly challenging profession, requiring loads of time and energy and testing every last nerve of its valiant chosen few from time to time. Most teachers know that the going will be tough when they enter the field and are prepared to sacrifice highly of themselves to help others. Tough challenges arise and test our mettle, but then recede into the past and perhaps leave us better off than we were before. No problem, really. Challenge is good. If teaching becomes a source of serious stress, however, further attention is needed. Look to what is driving your career to make sure your reasons for teaching are lined up right.

Practically speaking, every teaching position has a job description, or more likely, several. When we apply, a posted, public description initially attracts us and serves as a reference in our application submission and subsequent interviews. When we start teaching, we may find that the "real" daily job description is different than what we inferred from the posting. Subtler still is our own job description in our minds, those large, lofty things we intend to accomplish as professional educators. Whether we are teaching third-grade Language Arts, sixth-grade American History, or ninth-grade Info Tech, we all have central foci of what we intend to accomplish through our work. Those intentions may be the place to look if you are stressed out.

This is a personal quest, as every teacher will have different motivations, expectations for their realization, and reactions to the results. All of us can benefit by investigating these things. Even if teaching does not stress you out at all, this is worth your while. Clarify exactly what it is—in what may be grandiose terms—you are trying to accomplish in this profession. Be brutally honest and search thoroughly. You will probably find several answers, some of which may complement one another and perhaps others which seem far afield or even out of place. You may be surprised at some of the stuff you find in there. Again, the top priority for one person may not even make the list of another. No problem; keep going.

Given that there really are no objectively right or wrong reasons for starting or maintaining a teaching career, except *for you*, here are some examples that could go either way:

- I want to make a difference in the world.
- I want to share my passion with others.
- I want to instill discipline and life skills in our young citizens.
- I like to be in charge.

- I want to give back.
- I enjoy being the expert in the room.
- I was always told I could be a great teacher.
- I want to be like my teacher(s).
- I want to do way better than my teacher(s).
- I want to improve the education system in my community.

You may characterize some of the items on this list as clearly "good" reasons, and others as shockingly far from your priorities. Other teachers will see it differently. Just mind your own business on this one. Keep checking in on what is driving you, keep looking at it honestly, and keep aligning it with your daily work in a give-and-take relationship. Your central motivations for teaching can change, just as your detailed actions can change, as you bring them into harmony again and again.

KEY IDEAS:

- Pay attention to the challenges you face, and face them well.
- If you find yourself truly stressed out about teaching, review your motivations.

IF YOU ARE CONSISTENTLY THREE WEEKS BEHIND ON YOUR PAPERWORK, YOU CAN STAY RIGHT ON IT TOO

I once taught private music lessons to an adult student that came to our home. He was about 30 years old, had chosen to invest in these lessons, was certainly self-motivated, and drove himself to our place unlike my younger students who came with their parents. For some reason, though, he always arrived about ten minutes late. Always. You could set your watch by it. Every lesson he apologized politely for being late, and didn't mind if we still had to end the lesson at the regular time some days, depending on my schedule.

I found it a bit strange that such a motivated student would arrive late, but even more odd that he could do it so consistently—never two minutes or twenty, always ten. It made me realize that he could certainly arrive as consistently at whatever time he wished each week; he just had to choose to do so.

Teachers attend to a lot besides those precious moments we actually spend in the classroom. We go to meetings, serve on committees and workgroups, supervise and chaperone events, and, of course, push a lot of papers. Solid organization skills are important to making these secondary duties function well, but they do not automatically determine the timing with which we handle them. We can choose not only *how* we want to get things "off our desk and onto theirs" but also *when* we want to do it on a regular basis.

Everyone is different. Some people like to be right on top of every detail, occasionally even getting slightly ahead of themselves. Others like to leave a few things for tomorrow, building in some relaxing time today. Still others like to leave everything until the last minute, explaining that they work best under pressure. Take a good look at your own timing during task completion and make sure you are actually in control. If you can consistently stay three weeks behind on your paperwork, you can stay right on it too.

The real "paperwork," which really matters, is not so much the daily grind materials, but the assignments, pop quizzes, and tests that students submit. If we expect our formative assessments to actually improve student learning, we must return results, feedback, and suggestions to them at an appropriate time in the instructional cycle. "Appropriate" does not necessarily mean "right away," nor should it in many cases. However, the earlier we can finish our evaluation of student work the better, because (1) we are likely to give it our best attention when not under pressure and (2) it will be ready when the ideal moment does arrive to share it.

If we have a three-week backlog of non-instructional paperwork, we may slow down a faculty committee or mildly disappoint an administrator, both of which might behoove us to make a change. If we are delayed on student paperwork, though, we may be slowing down their growth, a possibility that is definitely worth our concern and contemplation. Test your natural tendencies for timing and determine what works best for you and your students. You may have more choice than you realize regarding what gets done when.

KEY IDEAS:

- All of us have our own truly best timing for getting work done well.
- Explore your task completion tendencies to make sure they are serving you and students.

EMBODY "ANYTHING IS POSSIBLE"
EVERY CHANCE YOU GET

Every teacher has been temporarily stuck, at one time or another, in the classroom. Some surprise creates what seems like a major obstacle to forward progress. The projector isn't working, the guest speaker didn't show up, the Internet is down, the student presenting this morning is sick at home, the teacher lost his voice, or a fire drill is eating class time when we need it most. On some days, it seems like all of the above happen at once. Within such trials lies a golden opportunity, though—discovering with your students what "anything is possible" might really mean.

> One of my star saxophone players approached me with bad news at the beginning of the school year. He needed to enroll in an AP course in his area of choice for college study, and it met at the same time as the advanced jazz band. He was heartbroken; so was I. Not so much because the ensemble would suffer or that the students would miss his presence or that we were counting on his leadership, but because he would miss out on an opportunity that we both knew he cherished. He did have room in his schedule to enroll in the intermediate jazz band but it would have been way too easy for him, not very educationally appropriate and somewhat of a waste of time, repeating material that he had already mastered. It was rather unfortunate that Matt would not have ideal opportunities for musical growth at school that semester.
>
> At the end of the term, all the bands were raring to go for their concert. The dress rehearsal went off without a hitch and all that was left was to get a good night's sleep and make it happen the following night. The next morning I received word that the top saxophone player in the intermediate band was in bed with a very high fever. He was definitely out for the next twenty-four hours or so. This was major news, as so many of our tunes depended on that particular player and his assigned parts.
>
> I quickly considered the option of tracking down a local professional to sit in as a "ringer," a fairly common solution in such situations. Then, I remembered Matt. I considered whether it was possible for him to come in and learn the charts on one brush-up rehearsal. Yes it was. Whether it was possible that the other students would rally around him and help him find his way quickly and successfully. Yes. Whether it was possible that this experience would be a great opportunity to learn some valuable skills that he could not have learned even within the original plan that was thwarted. Absolutely.
>
> The rest is history; Matt showed up and played great, I made brief comments to the audience about what was happening behind the scenes, everyone had a blast, and the concert was a success. I think everyone in the hall that night, certainly including me, took home our own little version of the personal reminder "Anything is possible."

It probably goes without saying that the more you face such challenges at school, the better you get at handling them effectively. What may come as a surprise, though, is that you may actually grow to *enjoy* them. It is possible that the longer you teach, and the more predictable things become every day, the happier you might be to field a surprise or two. More important, the greater the chances that your students will learn to plumb the depths of the possibility tank themselves.

> *I recently had a surprise comment from a college education major as he filed out after a challenging class. The projector wasn't syncing and I had used three or four different workarounds to solve the problem for three or four different activities that day. He said, "Sorry, I just had to tell you . . . . It seems like with most teachers when the technology goes down, instruction just stops. But you always seem to find a way to move on. I'm remembering that for my own teaching." I grinned and shot back "Great, because you'll need it!" as he went on his way.*

You never know which of your actions might make a difference in students' lives; let us strive to embody "anything is possible" every chance we get.

KEY IDEAS:

- Challenges and obstacles abound in the daily activities of classroom life.
- Embrace them as potentially refreshing opportunities to prove, again, that all is possible.

THERE IS NO SUBSTITUTE FOR QUICK THINKING

"Quick thinking" and "thinking on your feet" are phrases we hear often, useful in life in general and specifically when teaching. The ability to process effectively what is happening in front of us, and inside of us, is the bulk of our job in the classroom. The speed at which we do this can make the difference between excellent interactions and mediocre ones.

Not every interaction with students has to be quick; we need not hasten to find answers and responses nor maintain fast pacing at all times. Sometimes, a purposeful pause or relaxed tempo can help students absorb the material and transfer the ideas better. Ironically, though, intentional pauses and relaxed pacing often result from quick thinking by the teacher to recognize their usefulness in the moment. When we are thinking quickly, we are able to make decisions just as, or even a bit before, a need in the classroom becomes desperate.

Are you a relatively quick thinker? In general? Only when necessary or desired? Only under certain circumstances? Do you know others that you would call quick thinkers? Why so? Is it possible for people to improve the quickness of their thinking? Is it desirable? Think about these questions in relation to your own description of quick thinking, and with regard to examples of friends or colleagues that seem to embody it.

We very likely can improve our pace of quality thinking; the evidence is in the fact that we tend to "click" at different rates depending on the situations we encounter. In some conversations, with certain people regarding certain topics in certain circumstances, we may find ourselves staying right on top of the dialogue easily or perhaps even becoming a bit bored. In others, we are giving our absolute best just to keep up. In the first situation, our quick-thinking skills are not being challenged; in the second, we are right in the middle of boot camp.

This comparison suggests the first opportunity for quickening your thinking on a regular basis, that is, spend time with quick thinkers. Identify those people you know who always seem to be right on top of the topic with great ideas, clear and creative responses, and even enough time and comfort level to add in irony or humor. These are the people that cause you to notice you are thinking better and stronger in their presence, even when discussing mundane and simple topics. You can observe how they operate and take a few mental notes about what seems to work for them, but more important, just spend a lot of time with them mutually sharpening your skills.

Other practical examples of ways to quicken thinking skills relate to how we absorb information. For example, most online videos can be adjusted for speed, so you can watch a debate, speech, lecture, or documentary at 1.25×,

1.5×, or even 2× pace. Try some different speeds with different materials to discover how your brain feels as it absorbs the information. Another is PDF readers, which can be set to automatically scroll at various speeds. Try setting the speed just slightly past your comfort level, to push you to read and absorb quickly while avoiding distractions and lulls. With both videos and PDFs, you can always slow them back down, pause, or back up, so be willing to push your absorption rate as you progress.

Again, faster is not always better. In our modern world, what we and our students sometimes need most is more time and space to really attend to our work fully. However, the *ability* to think quickly can be so useful when just the right response or next move is needed. In the heat of the moment, there is no substitute. When you maneuver successfully through one of those moments, you'll be glad you practiced.

KEY IDEAS:

- Quick thinking can make appropriate, quality responses more likely.
- Practical ways to quicken your thinking are plentiful; put them to good use right now.

TAKE NONE OF THE CREDIT

Teachers have the right to be quite proud of our work. We are, after all, guiding the next generation of human beings to be fully functioning members of society, capable of carrying out their roles in their workplace and community in highly effective ways. Teachers are powerful people who assume a great deal of responsibility, and when things go well in our classrooms and schools we feel great. We have a choice, though, whether or not to take credit for the impressive things our students do. We should take this choice seriously each time it arises because it can profoundly influence how we function in the future.

If you decide to take the credit for school successes, you must also take the blame when things don't work out. You cannot have one without the other. Perhaps this feels fine to you; after all, it's just the way things really are, right? Take a moment to look a little deeper. Credit and blame exist only in your mind; in fact, even successes and failures exist only in your mind. Taking the credit and the blame for various situations is up to you, and both usually muddy the waters of what otherwise could be a clearer flow.

All of this really boils down to the sense of some internal person who is trying to keep track. Some entity seems to be in there trying to generate more successes than failures in your school life, that is, trying to have things go "right" or even "wonderfully" as often as possible. Sounds reasonable enough, right? The problem is that most of that is extraneous to student learning. It may indirectly create motivation to improve our classrooms, or to strive to do better, but mostly it complicates our teacher lives unnecessarily. It forces us into an attempt to keep a tally of wins and losses in our educational endeavors and to entertain a highly onerous bunch of personal baggage called reputation.

In contrast, when we let go of both the credit and the blame, both the successes and the failures, our attention can go straight to students. And stay there. We release ourselves and our students from such a strong attachment to results and instead focus fully on making the most of the learning process. The end becomes way less important than the means, a shift which tends to produce amazing ends anyway. Past successes and failures are given only the amount of attention useful to making the current activity go as well as possible, so pressure is reduced and performance improves. It is akin to a golfer leaving a difficult last hole, round, or entire tournament in the past so that today's play will be unaffected.

Letting go of taking the credit may seem like a noble, albeit difficult, thing to do; letting go of taking the blame seems like downright shirking of our duty. Are we to stop taking blame for things that are our fault? Of course not.

We should accept responsibility for mishaps openly, honestly, and publicly in front of our students and colleagues when appropriate, but we need not overdo it nor allow it to fester. How do we know when taking the blame is festering? We know when it begins to negatively affect our forward progress in the classroom. Students get over things quickly. We should too. Do what needs to be done and get moving again in the right direction.

KEY IDEAS:

- Taking the credit and taking the blame are in your mind, completely up to you.
- Consider whether either is actually helping your students in any way in a given moment.

KEEP THINGS FRESH

Like anything in life, teaching can become old hat. Against our greater wishes, and sometimes imperceptibly, the school day can gradually grow more and more predictable, classes of students seem to repeat themselves, and we may even question whether we have already covered a given topic or whether that happened last year. Our educational climate can become stale if we are not vigilant and proactive about keeping it fresh.

Relatively few things actually must stay the same from year to year at school. You might be assigned the same classroom with the same furniture and equipment. You might be teaching courses of the same name within a relatively static overarching curriculum. You might have the same colleagues in your department for a good long stretch of time. Even these relatively stable factors can be approached with fresh eyes and a creative spirit to keep things interesting.

What's more, there are a *host* of daily details you can change at will, anytime and as often as you like. For example,

- Your method of transportation to work.
- The route you take there.
- What, if anything, you listen to on your way in.
- What time you arrive.
- What you pack for lunch. And an extra snack? Tasty mid-morning beverage?
- Who you engage in conversation in the morning and at breaks.
- How you start each class.
- How you end each class.
- The lighting and ventilation in your room.
- Where you position yourself in class.
- How much you move during class.
- Your walking route from class to lunch or bus duty and back.
- Your attitude at faculty meetings.
- Your participation at faculty meetings.
- The frequency and tone of your communications to parents.
- The way you engage "school stuff" in the evening and on weekends.

Trying out options in categories like these not only helps us find our favorite solution for each but also can serve to make change just for the sake of making change periodically. Recognizing that there is a chance, even a slight one, that your approach to school can become stale, you do yourself a favor by proactively shifting your routine. In many cases, you will be the only one that actually knows you have made the change, but certainly not the only one to reap the benefits. For the good of your whole school community, keep things fresh in the little ways that are easily accessible to you.

KEY IDEAS:

- Teaching can become stale in a number of ways, sometimes imperceptibly.
- Make a habit of breaking your habits, especially when it will improve your environment.

WHEN YOU'RE IN IT FOR YOURSELF, TEACHING IS DIFFICULT; WHEN YOU'RE IN IT FOR OTHERS, IT'S EASY

It may seem crazy to suppose that teachers could be "in it for themselves." We have chosen, after all, one of the most important *service* positions society has to offer. We intend to give all we have to help the next generation grow up great. Yet there are quite a few attractive features of many teaching jobs—reasonable salary, health benefits, and summer vacation, for example—that we probably all have to admit we enjoy, and these things are direct benefits to us. The truth of the matter is probably that no teachers are completely in it for themselves, and no teachers are completely in it for others. Here, we begin our investigation.

Are there aspects of your job, or periods in the day or week, that you feel more of a focus on yourself than usual? Are you nervous about how many of "your" students will score 4's and 5's on their AP exam? Quickly tidying up your room and silently praying that your first graders will behave miraculously well when the principal comes to visit tomorrow? Excited yet frightened about how next week's art show will influence parents' perceptions of your teaching efficacy? These examples mostly indicate a focus on oneself, pointing out what you hope the results will ultimately do for you.

On the other hand, are there aspects of your job, or periods in the day or week, that you feel more of a focus on others than usual? Freely offering extra time prior to homeroom for anyone who needs help with world history, with no expectation for gratitude or acknowledgment? Developing a system of student leaders in class who will take on additional responsibilities but also absorb all of the credit for group progress? Identification of individual needs among students and creation of additional materials for differentiated instruction? These examples indicate a focus on others, pointing out what you hope the results will do for students.

Just reading the examples above probably brings up slight feelings of anxiety regarding the first group and feelings of strength and satisfaction from the second. Living them on a regular basis heightens those feelings exponentially. In those moments when you are focused on yourself, fighting for your rights, or concerned about your own interests, life at school can feel like a struggle or even a battle. When you give yourself over to others regularly and genuinely, life at school is rather harmonious and much easier.

Perhaps you are "in it for yourself" only very rarely, when it seems necessary, or perhaps that is the case most of the time. Maybe you are "in it for others" almost always, or you realize you could be more often. Take some time to identify additional examples throughout your day of relatively selfish and unselfish teacher moves, and the way you feel internally regarding those circumstances. You, of course, are the only one that can sense these things clearly and treat them honestly from within. Experiment with other options for how you might approach each situation, adjusting your frame of reference, introspection, and desired outcomes to discover what would make everything flow best for everyone. If you are hung up inside, your classroom will be too; if you are flowing generously and naturally inside, your classroom will be too. When you're in it for yourself, teaching can be difficult. When you're in it for others, it's really quite easy.

KEY IDEAS:

- We naturally experience relatively selfish and unselfish moments throughout the day.
- Paying attention to how your actions impact you internally can help you balance the two.

EXERCISE YOUR FREEDOMS

A common lament of many teachers is the sheer quantity of boundaries that surround our work. Federal legislation, state mandates, school district policy, local building procedures, legal paperwork, and scheduling conflicts all seem to box us in and limit our options. We enter the profession for the magic we can make with students only to find our own hands tied for the better part of the show. Discussion among colleagues frequently affirms these limits or even introduces us to new ones we did not realize were coming. In the midst of all the boundaries, though, there are freedoms. Every job has them, and teachers who exercise their freedoms will find they bring a great deal of job satisfaction.

Both the limits and the freedoms for any given teacher will be unique. Some teachers may brainstorm their limits and find they have relatively few. Others feel completely trapped. In either case, finding our freedoms is the best way to counteract, or simply balance, those imposed boundaries. This balance can help us maintain a healthy attitude, a consistent and helpful self-discipline, and a resourceful nature that benefits not only us but our students directly.

Here is a sample list of freedoms that you may or may not have at your disposal, to get you thinking about how you might maximize them:

- relatively ample contact time with students in a given course or courses;
- relatively wide curricular decision-making power in a course or courses;
- opportunities and resources to take students to off-campus learning experiences;
- more than one classroom space option at all times or on a given day of the week;
- autonomy regarding classroom atmosphere, rules, and logistics;
- opportunities to provide substantial input at faculty meetings;
- choices regarding which extracurricular activities you attend or sponsor;
- flexibility regarding what time you arrive to and leave school grounds on given days;
- options for where you take your prep period; and
- options for where you eat your lunch.

Relatively few teachers are enjoying all such factors at once, but probably all of us can find at least one item on the list that pertains to our particular job. The list generally proceeds from more crucial educational considerations to smaller, more personal ones, but something as simple as the last item could very well be the saving grace of your career. Even in the small details, the enjoyment of a bit of freedom can brighten your day and improve your outlook. Exercising those freedoms can also boost your self-discipline because you reaffirm some degree of autonomy in an increasingly prescriptive environment. You really do have the power to make a lot of choices every day at school, and the more of them you make proactively, the greater the personal momentum you generate.

Your resourcefulness in exercising freedoms also can have a profound impact on students. If your fourth-period class recognizes that you were squeezed out of the normal classroom by necessity, but managed to find an even better space through some innovative thinking, they might just be inspired by your ability to make things happen. Inspired by your freedom to go ahead and make things better. By your freedom to see all your options. Your freedom to find satisfaction and bring enjoyment to everything you do. Your freedom to exercise your freedoms.

KEY IDEAS:

- Educational environments may contain a great many limits by multiple sources.
- Finding the freedoms therein and exercising them fully can inspire us and our students.

IT'S OKAY TO ENJOY YOUR JOB

Strangely enough, there seems to be a culture in some school faculties of mild distaste for the work we have chosen. Teachers won't actually say this directly (well, some might) but their words and actions speak loud and clear—they don't seem to be enjoying their job. Complaints abound, gossip spreads, conflicts arise, tension builds, exhaustion ensues—the stuff of teachers' lounge lore. Some relatively healthy, balanced teachers—especially newer ones—may be led to believe that this is how teaching is, a highly onerous, relatively thankless, long-distance trudge of a career. Don't be deceived; it's okay to enjoy your job.

It is amazing how a school culture can affect a new recruit, for better or for worse. A great way to approach your own teaching career, no matter how long you've been at it, is to actively seek out those colleagues and circumstances that are likely to contribute to your enjoyment of the job rather than your dissatisfaction with it. Chances are there is at least one person, if not many, many more, who will be glad to reciprocally pitch in a bit of help or humor on a daily basis to make the workplace more pleasant.

We often use "enjoy" to mean taking joy or pleasure from something, but the word originally meant putting joy into it. Rather than split hairs on the definition, why not go for both? They work great together. Put a bit of joy into what you do and chances are you'll take a lot of joy out of it too.

We encounter myriad reasons to be grateful, joyful, and content throughout the school day. So, why not do it? This does not mean we ignore the troubles or slacken in our work ethic; teaching is certainly a highly challenging career, but we can bring joy even to the trials and tribulations. It all depends on our approach. We can either complain about a situation, resisting in our mind what is happening and insisting that it shouldn't be that way, or dive in with hope and determination to make a change to the best of our ability. In the end, it is really up to each of us whether we enjoyed our work or not, and our decision will show up in the way we relate it to others.

Take a good look at those aspects of your teaching position that you consider most difficult to enjoy. Paperwork? Disciplinary action? Meetings? Bus duty? Parent conferences? In-services? Third period? What is it that you find yourself complaining about, even if only mildly and perhaps to yourself? What is it that holds you back from going ahead and enjoying those aspects of the job instead? Are they *inherently* unenjoyable? Would it be impossible for *anyone* to enjoy that particular part? Do you find that *everyone* at your school hates that aspect of their work unanimously? If so, it might be worth proposing some change as a faculty body. If not, look to those people who are the exceptions to see how they bring joy to that facet of the daily grind, and find that joy in yourself. It's actually not that hard to do.

The beginning of this essay painted a fairly bleak picture of some school faculties' typical functioning. Maybe your collective colleagues are already in pretty good shape regarding work enjoyment. If so, keep it up and be grateful. If you find a lot of dissatisfaction and unhappiness among some or many of your colleagues, though, don't lose heart. It's totally up to you; you can even enjoy the process of learning how to enjoy your job. Start right now.

KEY IDEAS:

- Your job satisfaction is up to you.
- Some aspects of our jobs may seem difficult to enjoy; find ways to enjoy them anyway.

IT IS NOT ABOUT YOU

A quick glance at an empty classroom suggests that two camps exist within the space. A large desk, file organizer, computer monitor, screen, and instructional props stand facing all those rows of desks or chairs. Tomorrow, the teacher will face the students.

Setups vary, of course. Some classrooms may feature several clusters of student chairs circled around small tables or a large semicircle of desks, but they all still seem to counterbalance the teacher's side of the room. The way these rooms are set up might just reflect the perceived relationship between teacher and students, a relationship which tends to place high importance on you in the overall classroom dynamic. We know deep down, though, that school exists for students, not for teachers. It is not about you.

You might ask yourself a few questions right now to determine how much you currently think that all of this is about you or not. Be honest with yourself as you explore "Do I get nervous about students' potential reception of me as an educator?," "Am I trying to make my family, my mentors, my colleagues, or my administrators proud of me and my fine teaching?," "Do I feel fulfilled having chosen a career in which I am making a difference in the world?," and "Am I striving to receive high marks from periodic administrator evaluations or students' feedback?" Some or all of these questions might seem rather innocent and reasonable at first glance, but all of them are about *you*, and all of them can detract from your attention to *your students*. Take a few moments to discover whether you have any of your own questions to be asked along these same lines.

Realizing that it is not about you is perhaps the most fundamental shift that happens as students become teachers. For most of our school-student lives, we learned that it is all about me: my grades, my progress, my behavior, my ideas, my performance, my contributions to group work, my strengths, my weaknesses, and my educational experience. Teachers encouraged us to self-reflect and self-assess, to remain acutely aware of our actions and the consequences they may bring. As high schoolers decide to become teachers and enter collegiate training programs they encounter more of the same: my coursework, my lesson plans, my peer teaching, my contributions to class discussion, my state exam scores, and my student teaching experience. All of these elements can spark and sustain our growth as experts in our subject matter and masters of the ways we convey it to others. As we transition fully into teaching, though, "we" must also learn to disappear. That is, the focus on ourselves we have learned so thoroughly through school must gradually dissolve into a full focus on our students.

Would it be possible to do what you do as a teacher a bit more anonymously? To forget about yourself altogether as you engage in a student interaction? To question who exactly this "I" is that receives so much attention as you plan for tomorrow or reflect on yesterday?

As your attention gradually shifts more fully from yourself to your students you may witness some simple but powerful changes in your room. Things seem to flow more freely, time moves swiftly and beautifully, and students become more active and engaged. These are natural consequences of your increasing ability to focus all of the energy, creativity, and attention available to you onto what the students are doing rather than what you are doing.

A common worry emerges if and when you determine to make this shift, that is, a genuine concern that you will "mess up" your part of planned teacher-student interactions if you choose to "forget" yourself for their sake. Remember that it is a process. This sort of shift does not have to happen overnight. Start with little bits of instruction that are *well* within your comfort zone, and experiment with how you can shift your attention back and forth between yourself and your students on the spot.

For example, reviewing basic spelling conventions on the screen at the front of the room may be more effortless for you than diagramming complex sentences under the same circumstances. In the first scenario, you find that you can attend almost completely to the students while you do your work automatically at the screen, while in the second scenario you have to focus more on what *you* are actually doing so that you accomplish it correctly. You may even entertain a thought or two along the way such as "I need to get this right, so they have a good example to remember" or even "I need to get this right so they know that I am good at this."

At that point, it is about you. Not helpful. First, take advantage of the opportunity to explore, internally, what it feels like to shift your focus freely when in your comfort zone (spelling review) to then be able to apply the same approach to other situations (diagramming) later. You may be surprised at the number of thoughts and feelings you observe within just a few moments' worth of being "on the spot" in front of students. Sorting this out and remembering, again and again, that it is not about you may be tough work, but you owe it to your students.

KEY IDEAS:

- Focus on ourselves is helpful during training, but can detract from attention to students.
- Keep experimenting with the focal shift from self to students in the heat of the moment.

About the Author

Nathan O. Buonviri is associate professor of Music Education at Temple University in Philadelphia. He has published in the top research journals in his field, and has presented papers and workshops across the United States and around the world on music education and teacher education. He has taught music, Spanish, reading comprehension, phonics, and math to students of all ages.